Get Into
UK Medical School 2015

The comprehensive
step-by-step guide
for success in applying to
UK medical school

Emma Owen

Contents

About the Book 1

Is Medicine right for me? 3
Deciding to become a doctor 4
Free medical school taster sessions 4
Medlink courses 6
Work placements 7
School medical societies 9
Books and blogs 10
Find out more about being a doctor 11
The right qualities for Medicine 13
Good communication skills 14
Good practice 14

Academic Requirements 16
GCSEs 17
AS and A levels 18
Extended Project Qualification 23

Work Experience 25
Why you need work experience 26
How much work experience is enough 26
Organising your placement 28
Preparing for your placement 29
What to do on your placement 30
After your placement 32

Voluntary Work & Employment 34
Volunteering 35
How to organise voluntary work 37
Getting the most out of volunteering 38

Volunteering abroad..39
Fundraising & charity work 40
Paid employment..41

Extra-curricular Activities...............................44
Being an all-rounder..45
Getting the wow factor..47
Writing a blog..47

Choosing a University......................................49
University Choices..50
Teaching methods..50
Problem Based Learning (PBL)................................51
Lecture-based courses 52
Tutorials and supervisions 52
Subject or systems based teaching..........................53
Traditional or integrated courses 54
Spiral courses...55
Intercalated degree 55
Student Selected Components 57
Anatomy..58
Elective 59
Admissions process 59
Location 61
Accommodation..62
Open Days..63
League tables 66

Admissions Tests 67
Why you need to take a test 68
The BMAT...70
What is in the BMAT...71
How the BMAT is scored..72
How universities use the BMAT................................73

ii

Practice questions & suggested reading 74
The UKCAT 75
UKCAT preparation 76
The UKCAT format 76
Verbal reasoning 77
Quantitative reasoning 78
Abstract reasoning 80
Decision analysis 81
Situational judgement 81
Useful UKCAT resources 82
Booking your UKCAT 84
The day of the test 85
Taking the test 86
Getting your result 87
How universities use the UKCAT 88

Your UCAS Application 91
UCAS 92
Your personal statement 93
Start early 95
Make it personal 95
The first draft 96
Edit 99
Submit it early 101
Your school reference 102

Important Background Knowledge 106
Know your facts 107
NHS 107
GMC 109
Tomorrow's Doctors 110
BMA 111
NICE 111
The Francis report 112

iii

Ethics 113
Ethical dilemmas 114
Autonomy and competence 115
Beneficence 116
Non-maleficence 117
Justice 117
Confidentiality 117

Preparing for an Interview 118
Why you will be interviewed 119
Waiting 120
Preparation 121
Background reading 121
Interview questions 124
The most commonly asked questions 126
Practising 130
Structuring your answers 131
Being positive & selling yourself 132
Using your personal statement 132
Answering the question 133

The Actual Interview 134
Getting an Interview 135
The night before your interview 135
The morning of the interview 136
When you get there 137
Body language 139
Appearing confident 141
Multiple Mini Interviews (MMIs) 143

After The Interview 149
Waiting for the result 150
Coping with rejection 150
Getting an offer 152

Health assessment and disclosure 153
Applying for funding 154
Scholarships and bursaries 156
Paying the money back 157
Getting the grades 157
Exam results 158
You made it! 159

Appendix 1 160
Suggested timeline 160

Appendix 2 163
Medical school GCSE requirements 163

Appendix 3 172
How universities use the UKCAT 172

Appendix 4 178
Useful university contact information 178

About the Book

Getting into a UK medical school is tougher than ever but this book will greatly increase your chances of successfully winning an offer.

It contains a wealth of the latest information, top tips and practical help to answer all your questions and guide you through the whole application process. With advice on what to do from first deciding you want to be a doctor, to making your UCAS application stand out and nailing the admissions tests, this book will enable you to shine in the all-important interview and finally win a coveted place at medical school.

Apart from the obvious academic criteria to study medicine, potential medics need to possess certain personal attributes such as an ability to empathise, excellent listening and communication skills, patience, organisational skills, an ability to lead and be part of a team, as well as mechanisms to cope under pressure. This book will help you to showcase these skills so that you excel at every stage of the process and ultimately achieve your goal to get into medical school.

From making sure you have the required grades at GCSE, the right A levels and suitable work experience, to writing the best personal statement and standing out in interviews, this book will guide you every step of the way.

With links to many of the most useful websites on your journey through the application process and contributions from a first year medical student who has just succeeded on that journey, this book has the most up-to-date information and shares with you the wisdom and secrets that other medical school application books leave out.

With this book, you CAN get into medical school!

Chapter 1

Is Medicine right for me?

Deciding to become a doctor 4
Free medical school taster sessions 4
Medlink courses 6
Work placements 7
School medical societies 9
Books and blogs 10
Find out more about being a doctor 11
The right qualities for Medicine 13
Good communication skills 14
Good practice 14

Deciding to become a doctor

Few people decide by the age of five that they want to be a doctor. For most, the decision is much harder and if there are no doctors in your family it may be difficult to really understand what being a doctor involves.

If you are basing your decision solely on a particular TV programme you enjoy watching then you may be in for a nasty shock. Even the fly-on-the-wall medical documentaries are edited in such a way to glamorise the profession. Neither should you think that a few visits to your GP during your childhood are an accurate representation of what a doctor does. You really need as much first-hand and varied experience of different medical specialties as possible to get an accurate idea of what lies ahead.

There are several ways that you can gain a true understanding of what life as a medic is really like, from taster courses and work experience in a medical setting to reading the right books and blogs and how you can find out more is outlined below.

Free medical school taster sessions

There are many opportunities for students who are either from state schools, low-income households or who have no family history of higher education to attend medicine taster sessions at their local university.

The university usually covers the cost of transport, food and activities and there may also be an opportunity to apply for a scholarship to their medical school if you are eligible.

During the taster sessions, which usually take place during the spring or summer holidays in year 12, students experience life as a university student by living and sleeping on campus for several days and nights, taking part in a variety of medicine seminars and social activities and receiving advice and guidance on applying to study medicine.

Look up opportunities available in your area but be aware that they are usually heavily over-subscribed and you may have to meet certain academic and geographical criteria, so do your research as soon as you can. A few examples are East Anglia University's Medical Aspirations programme, Queen Mary's spring and summer school programme and Cambridge University's Sutton Trust summer school programme. Links to these are listed below, however, there is likely to be something similar close to you so have a look to see what is available in your area.

http://www.uea.ac.uk/study/info-for/young-people/post-16/university-tasters-enrichment/medical-aspirations

http://www.qmul.ac.uk/undergraduate/schools/educationliaison/wp/summerschools/index.html

http://www.study.cam.ac.uk/undergraduate/access/year12summerschool/info.html

Medlink courses

If you are not eligible for a free taster course, there are still plenty of ways to find out if medicine is the right career for you and one way is to attend a course like the ones run by Medlink. These are very popular with Year 12 students and generally take place at the end of the first term in year 12 (Medlink), during the Easter holidays (Medisix) or in July (Medsim).

The courses offer you the opportunity to stay at a university in a hall of residence for 3-5 days with other like-minded students where you will attend a series of useful lectures and fun practical sessions run by doctors. Although it is not cheap (about £200 for 3 days), it is a great way to find out more about medicine and gives you a real taste of what medical school will be like.

Sessions include: The Edge, Applying to Oxbridge, How to get an A* in Chemistry, Clinical skills and an optional Pathology day where there is an opportunity to do a research project and get it published. You also get a free stethoscope which you learn to use and can wear round your neck like a real doctor!

You can find out more at the following websites:

http://medlink-uk.net/conference/

http://medblog.medlink-uk.net

'I attended a five day Medlink course at Nottingham University and it really motivated me to apply to medical school. There was a particular lecture called The Edge which was the highlight for most people as the speaker, James Ridgeway, gave lots of tips to help with the application process.

Everybody that I met there felt it was well worth the money and I made lots of friends who I am still in touch with through the free Medlink blogging site and other social networking sites. It also ticked a box on my Duke of Edinburgh Gold Award as it counted towards my residential part of the award so that was a bonus!' – 1st year medical student.

Work placements

If a residential course is not possible or affordable, don't worry because there are other ways to find out what it is like to be a doctor. Firstly, don't be afraid to exploit even the remotest contacts if you have any. Now is definitely the time to call your aunt whose brother-in-law is an ENT specialist to see if she can fix you up with a few days shadowing. You have nothing to lose and you'll probably find that most doctors will be flattered to be asked to show round a prospective medical student. They can probably arrange for you to shadow colleagues in other specialties too.

If you are not lucky enough to know anybody in your immediate circle of friends or family then check on the website of your local hospital for any work experience placements. Look under the 'Work for us' section, which will guide you through the application.

'I went to my local hospital for a week in July on an Aspiring Doctors Programme for sixth form students hoping to go into medicine. It was an excellent opportunity to see lots of different specialties but the highlight for me was being allowed to watch a three-hour open bowel surgery on one of the hottest days of the year and not fainting.' – 1st year medical student.

Although it is not often possible to do a work placement at your local GP surgery because of patient confidentiality issues, your GP may be able to spend time with you outside of office hours to discuss their work or they may be able to set you up with a placement at another GP surgery. However, remember that GPs are incredibly busy so do not expect them to do more than give you a contact name and number. If you are lucky enough to be accepted on a placement at a surgery then the patients will have to grant you permission before you are allowed to sit in on their consultations.

Finally, if you find it difficult to find a suitable placement, ask your teachers, as they should have details of work experience that previous students did for their medical school applications.

School medical societies

If your school has a medical society this is a good way of learning more about medicine. School societies are usually run by sixth-formers wishing to study medicine and they involve regular talks by outside speakers from different fields of medicine. If your school already has a medical society try to take an active part in it and even offer to run it when the current leader leaves. This is an opportunity to show that you are a good team player with leadership skills and it will also provide you with something to talk about in interview.

If your school doesn't have a medical society this is the perfect opportunity for you to start one up and it will look good on your personal statement, as it will show that you are creative, motivated and independent! As long as you have the support of your Head and a handful of interested students from years 11 - 13 then all you have to do is decide who your first guest will be. Write a polite letter introducing yourself and make your request. Don't forget to offer refreshments and travel reimbursements as well as power-point facilities and a variety of possible dates and times.

'In my school MedSoc we arranged talks from medical students, medical admissions tutors, consultants and professors. This actually came up as a role-play scenario in a medical school interview so first-hand experience of organising something like this is really useful.' – 1st year medical student.

Books and blogs

Try to read as many books or blogs as you can about life as both a medical student and doctor. Some recommended books are:
- *Trust Me I'm a (Junior) Doctor* by Max Pemberton
- *In Stitches – The Highs and Lows of Life as an A&E Doctor* by Dr Nick Edwards
- *Bedside Stories: Confessions of a Junior Doctor* by Michael Foxton
- *Confessions of a GP* by Dr Benjamin Daniels.

These four books are all well-written, entertaining accounts of real life working in the NHS and are suitable reading for any potential medical student.

Bad Science by Ben Goldacre takes a look at the bad science behind some of the dodgy headlines in the media including the MMR scare and other 'scientific breakthroughs' and is useful reading for background information about issues that may be asked in an interview.

Cancer Ward by Aleksandr Solzhenitsyn is an interesting book to read if you are also studying A Level History as it is not only a compassionate study of terminally ill patients but also describes the cancerous Soviet police state in Cold War Russia.

You can also read a selection of blogs by Medlink members at: http://medblog.medlink-uk.net/blogs/

Find out more about being a doctor

The reality of being a doctor is a lifetime of learning, which doesn't finish when you leave university. You will start by spending between 4 and 6 years at medical school depending on whether you enter as an undergraduate or postgraduate. During this time you will learn about the anatomy of the human body, how to diagnose and treat diseases and what is required for a person to keep healthy. Many universities offer an extra year of study, usually in the 3rd or 4th year, for you to do some research and gain an intercalated degree. Nottingham University, however, uniquely include this within their 5 year course.

Every medical school has to cover the same teaching material, but each school will have their own particular style of teaching, which you can read about in the 'Choosing a University' chapter starting on page 49. However, wherever you go, you will be taught through a variety of lectures, seminars, tutorials, laboratory sessions and eventually hospital placements.

When you have completed your medical degree you will be ready to start your on-the-job training and will have a medical qualification, for example MB ChB. The medical qualifications can be confusing; the letters 'MB' stand for 'Bachelor of Medicine' while the letters 'ChB' stand for 'Bachelor of Surgery'. However there is no difference between MB ChB and other medical degrees, for example MBBS or MB BCh.

When you graduate from university you will get a provisional licence from the General Medical Council (GMC) to practice as a junior doctor for 2 years. These are your 2 foundation years and you will start earning a basic salary from about £22,000 that increases to about £28,000 in your second foundation year. During this time you will be constantly training in an ever-evolving subject and you will have to keep up with all the new advancements in medicine. You will be able to assess, diagnose and manage the treatment of patients and will have to cope with working long hours. After this you have the choice of further training, either in General Practice or a hospital speciality, which could take from between 3 and 8 years before you reach consultant level. Other options are to move into research or lecturing if you do not want to work directly with patients.

It is therefore crucial that you are well informed with a realistic view of medicine and are passionate about becoming a doctor and that you are not doing it just to please someone else like a parent or teacher.

Look at these websites for more information about a career in medicine:

http://www.gmc-uk.org

https://www.medicalcareers.nhs.uk/considering_medicine/introduction.aspx

The right qualities for Medicine

Now you have researched and found out if medicine is right for you, you need to ask yourself some soul-searching questions to find out if you are right for medicine. Being a doctor is not just about excelling academically and having an interest in science. Good doctors must possess the qualities and attributes that instil trust both in their patients and others in the profession, so ask yourself the following questions and try to answer honestly:

- *Are you a caring and compassionate person?*
- *Are you a good listener?*
- *Can you explain things easily so that others understand?*
- *Are you honest and trustworthy?*
- *Do you empathise with others?*
- *Can you cope well in stressful situations?*
- *Are you patient?*
- *Do you have common sense?*
- *Are you practical and hands-on?*
- *Do you mind working long hours?*
- *Do you work well in a team?*
- *Are you a leader?*
- *How much do you really want to be a doctor?*

If you answered yes to most of these then you have the sort of qualities that are required of medics. However, if you answered no to any of them, you should seriously reconsider why you want to study medicine, as you will be unlikely to get through the rigorous admissions procedures.

Good communication skills

Good communication is not just about being a good public speaker; someone that can put together some good arguments and make people believe in what they are saying, nor is it just about being good at explaining things clearly. The most important communication skill a doctor can have is to be a good listener.

Doctors often need to get their patients to open up and talk about what is wrong with them, which can be difficult sometimes. It is important to practice asking open-ended questions and then to wait for the other person to answer in their own time. Don't be tempted to answer for them or to assume you know how they feel.

Good practice

Becoming a doctor is not only a career choice but a lifestyle choice too. You will always be expected to adhere to professional standards even outside the workplace, which includes how you present yourself on social networking sites.

If your email account has a wacky name now might be a good time to set up a new more professional email account for future correspondence with university tutors and future employers.

Remember that if you post photos or comments on Facebook, Twitter etc. that they may be seen and read by future employers or patients. Use your common sense and don't participate in silly Internet crazes that may come back to haunt you one day.

University students often have a reputation for heavy partying but the GMC does not look kindly on illegal drug taking for example, so behave appropriately at all times.

'Students must be aware that their behaviour outside the clinical environment, including in their personal lives, may have an impact on their fitness to practice. Their behaviour at all times must justify the trust the public places in the medical profession.' – GMC

Look at the following websites for more information about good practice:

http://www.gmc-uk.org/education/undergraduate/professional_behaviour.asp

http://www.gmc-uk.org/education/undergraduate/tomorrows_doctors.asp

Chapter 2

Academic Requirements

GCSEs 17
AS and A levels 18
Extended Project Qualification 23

GCSEs

Whatever stage you are at your journey to medical school really starts in Year 10 when you choose your GCSE options. Most medical schools will want to see that you have studied all three sciences at GCSE level and have the top grades in at least 7 subjects, including Maths, English Language, English Literature and the three sciences, Biology, Chemistry and Physics.

The requirements vary between universities but generally you will need to prove that you are more than academically able to study medicine. Remember that medicine is a very competitive subject and most applicants will have an armful of top grades. This doesn't mean that you have to have 13 A*s; in fact many universities only consider your top 7 grades and disregard the others, meaning that it is far better to concentrate on getting those crucial A*/A grades in the most important subjects mentioned above.

However, be aware that these are the minimum requirements for GCSE and the competition is tough, so it is important to check now that you have the right grades in the right subjects in case you need to have a rethink about your decision to study medicine.

There are plenty of other health care courses out there that are less demanding academically such as nursing, physiotherapy and occupational therapy.

If your GCSE results were disappointing but you still want to be a doctor, you could choose to study a similar subject to medicine like bio-medical science and enter medicine as a postgraduate where your degree will matter more than your GCSE results. Whatever your situation there are ways to get into medical school as long as you do the research and stay determined.

A limited number of places on access courses are available at most universities for students from disadvantaged backgrounds or poorly performing schools. If you think you might be eligible then go to the individual medical school websites for more information.

See Appendix 1 for a typical timeline for applying to medical school and Appendix 2 for the latest GCSE requirements for all the medical schools taken from their websites. (Note that these websites are constantly under review so do check that the information is still correct.)

AS and A levels

AS and A2 choices are important for any degree course but especially for medicine. Almost all medical schools require that you have studied Chemistry and at least one other science subject (either Biology, Physics or Maths) at Advanced level.

Some universities which request chemistry at Advanced level include Dundee, Edinburgh, Glasgow, Hull York, Lancaster, Liverpool, and Manchester while a few universities insist on both Chemistry and Biology to be studied to A2, including Hull York, Lancaster, Liverpool and Nottingham.

There are, however, a few medical schools that do not require Chemistry at A2. The university of East Anglia stipulates that you must have either Biology or Human Biology and one other science from either Chemistry or Physics. Other universities offer the option of studying either Chemistry or Biology but not necessarily both to A2. These include Durham, Imperial, Kings and Newcastle.

Some of the more traditional universities will expect you to have studied at least 3 sciences at A level so if you really want to study at universities like Oxford or Cambridge for example, you will need to have all science A levels (Chemistry, Biology, Physics or Maths).

However, other universities may look favourably on a 3rd. non-science subject such as History, which shows that you have a flair for essay writing and deductive skills, both useful attributes for making diagnoses. Some medical schools even prefer applicants who study contrasting subjects as it shows a rounded individual. It is most important to choose subjects that you enjoy as well as being good at as you will be spending a great deal of time studying them over the next two years.

Do make sure that your A level choices are not too similar though. For example, if you study Maths and Further Maths at A level, universities usually count them as one subject or only recognise Further Maths at AS level. This is the same with Biology and Human Biology so make sure you check your choices are eligible for medicine by looking at the entry requirements on the medical school websites of the universities. General Studies is generally not considered as a full A or AS level by the majority of medical schools so to be safe don't include it as one of your 4 subjects.

Some people decide to take 4 or more subjects at Advanced level but this is not necessary and might actually be more detrimental than just taking 3 subjects. Medical schools are looking for top grades and it is far better to achieve AAA than AABB. For instance Imperial College London requests AAAC if you are offering 4 subjects at A2.

If you are unsure whether to take 4 subjects or not, consider the option that it might be better to use your extra time to volunteer or do work experience, as these non-academic pastimes can be just as important as top grades to securing a place at medical school.

However, if you believe you have the time and capability to perform well in all 4 subjects at Advanced level, then you are sure to impress admissions tutors especially at some of the more academic medical schools.

With AS levels it is even more important to perform well than in your GCSEs as most schools and/or colleges use your attainment in your AS subjects as the basis for your A2 predicted grades; which are a significant criterion for entry to medical school.

It is often common practice for medical schools to reject an application if the predicted grades do not reach the minimum entry requirements. The minimum grade of your 4th AS level/'dropped' A Level is also sometimes specified (often grade B), so be sure to work hard in all of your subjects even if you are intending to drop one.

You need to ensure that your teachers will make good A2 level predictions in your reference for your UCAS application form. The best way to do this is to make sure that you perform really well at AS level and try to get top grades if possible.

It's true you can retake modules the following year but it's far better to put in the effort in year 12. You have to send in your AS results on your UCAS form and there is so much competition that you need to make sure you're at least as good as the rest.

Most universities request your first result, not your re-sit, and they don't count exams taken in a different year. So try to keep on top of your work, especially coursework.

Remember, if you want to be a doctor you'll need to be well organised and manage your time well so it's best to start now. If your teachers see you working hard and getting work in on time, they are also more likely to write you a good reference, which is crucial to your application.

If, however, you have some extenuating circumstances during your A levels, like a family bereavement or illness, which make your work and grades suffer, then make sure that your teachers are aware of the situation and explain it in your school reference on your UCAS application.

If you wait until you have your A2 results and then try to explain disappointing results on extenuating circumstances, it may be too late and the universities may not take them into account. Your teachers should also let the exam boards know about extenuating circumstances when you sit your exams as many of them will offer up to 5% extra marks as a special consideration.

So choose subjects that you enjoy as well as ones that are suitable for entry to medical school, do your best and try not to worry about your examinations, as there are ways of working round results if they're not quite what you expect.

Extended Project Qualification

The Extended Project Qualification or EPQ is a piece of independent work usually examined by either AQA or Edexcel which tests students' critical, reflective, problem-solving and independent learning skills through the planning, research and evaluation of a chosen project. The EPQ is graded from A* to E and takes approximately 120 guided learning hours after which students receive a qualification equivalent to half an A level (up to a maximum of 70 UCAS points).

If you decide to do the EPQ you'll need to write a 5,000 word dissertation or produce either an investigation, performance or artefact with a 1,000 word report. You will also have to deliver a presentation between 10 and 15 minutes long about your topic to an audience.

http://www.aqa.org.uk/programmes/aqa-baccalaureate/extended-project/the-aqa-epq

If you can't wait to research a particular topic then go for it. It will help to set you apart from the other straight A applicants as long as you can show what you have learnt along the way. It could also prove your commitment to a subject and allow you to develop the independent research skills needed for study at university. If you are lucky enough to receive an interview it could give you something to talk about, so when you choose a topic try to make it medically or health related.

UCL says, '*The EPQ can provide useful preparation for undergraduate study in terms of undertaking research, writing up a project and making a presentation. Students may also find that the EPQ allows them the opportunity to enjoy researching an area of particular interest and it may provide a useful topic for discussion during interviews. We would encourage students to consider taking the EPQ if it is offered at their school. Students who have chosen to take all science and mathematics subjects at A-level may wish to undertake the EPQ in order to demonstrate a broader skill set, but we would also welcome the EPQ being offered by students who do offer contrasting subjects at A/AS-level.*'

However, although gaining an A* in an EPQ will look good on your personal statement and provide possible discussion material in an interview, it does not form part of the entry criteria for any of the medical schools so it is not necessary to do one to get in.

Think carefully before starting one as you're going to be incredibly busy studying for your three As at A level, as well as all the other extra-curricular activities you have to do and it can be a big and perhaps unnecessary commitment.

Many schools don't actually start teaching the EPQ until Year 13 so unless you are absolutely certain that you will complete it, don't mention it on your personal statement as you may be asked about it in an interview six months later.

Chapter 3

Work Experience

Why you need work experience 26
How much work experience is enough 26
Organising your placement 28
Preparing for your placement 29
What to do on your placement 30
After your placement 32

Why you need work experience

Many medicine applicants don't realise that work experience is just as important, if not more than achieving the highest grades in exams. Unlike other subjects medicine is more than just a degree; it is a career and a future way of life so medical school admissions tutors are looking for students who have a thorough understanding of what life as a doctor is like. The only way that you can really show that you understand what it entails is by completing as much work experience as possible in a relevant health care setting. It's no good if you go through the whole application process only to find that you can't stand the sight of blood when you get to medical school!

In medical school interviews you will be treated as a potential doctor so you must be able to demonstrate an understanding of what doctors do.

How much work experience is enough

It's not what you do but what you do with it! The amount of work experience or shadowing opportunities you do doesn't matter as long as you make the most of whatever you do so don't worry if you can only organise a day or two here and there. Only a few universities, such as Nottingham, will ask you to list dates and times you spent at different places; in fact it is definitely not recommended to list your placements like a badge of honour on your personal statement.

It is far more important to have a few anecdotes about things you saw, did or thought about while you were observing than a list of hospitals or specialties you went to.

Having said that, the more opportunities you have to experience a variety of placements the better, as you will have a broader selection of experiences to discuss in an interview. Also, by organising different placements you are showing your commitment to medicine, and it is one of the main ways universities distinguish between candidates' motivation.

Dundee Medical School - *'Applicants are expected to demonstrate some knowledge of, and commitment to, medicine. Thus we encourage up to two weeks of medically-related work or shadowing experience.'*

In general, most applicants will have spent between 2 and 4 weeks shadowing over a year or two. Due to the pressure of exams it is best to try to organise your work experience as early in the process as possible.

The summer holidays after Year 11 are a good time to start, however many hospitals will not take students who are under 16, so bear this in mind when planning your placement.

The October and February half terms in Year 12 are also a good time to do a few days, but it is probably best to leave the Easter holidays for revision as it can be mentally and physically exhausting to do both.

Organising your placement

If you are lucky enough to know a doctor who has agreed to let you shadow them, it is polite to give them as much notice as possible beforehand. Although they may have agreed to let you follow them around the hospital there is almost always likely to be a strict protocol that you will have to adhere to. It is best, once you have agreed the dates with the doctor you are shadowing, to get in touch with the work experience coordinator at the hospital so that they can send you any paperwork that needs completing before you start.

Some hospitals will insist on seeing proof that you have had certain vaccinations like MMR before you will be allowed on wards, so ask your GP whom to contact for a copy of all your vaccination records.

It is unlikely that you will have to have a DBS (formerly CRB) check before you start as you should never be left unsupervised on your placement, however you should disclose any criminal convictions you may have had.

You may find that you have to complete a theatre orientation session if you are planning to watch an operation and these may only be available on certain days. Don't be surprised if you have to sign a confidentiality form before you start either.

If you are hoping to be accepted on a set work experience programme at your local hospital, then it is likely that you will have to apply for a place several months before the programme commences. You can check this out on the hospital website but bear in mind that places are very limited on these programmes and there will be a lot of competition, so make sure you apply early and treat your application as seriously as your UCAS application as it is good practice for later.

Preparing for your placement

You will usually be given an induction before you begin your placement so that you know what to expect and are fully prepared and informed before you start. Remember you will be working alongside health professionals whose primary concern is patient safety so it is essential that you act in a professional manner at all times and are punctual and reliable.

You will be expected to be dressed appropriately which usually means nothing to be worn below the elbow, including nail varnish and jewellery. Any visible tattoos should be covered with a sticking plaster and unusual piercings removed. Trainers and open toe sandals are not usually permitted and long hair should be tied back. You will probably be asked to wear a visible ID badge at all times and may be asked to sign a confidentiality form, so if you write about your experience afterwards remember to maintain patient confidentiality and do not disclose patients' identities.

It may be a good idea to jot down any preconceptions, concerns or hopes that you have before you start your placement. This will help you later when you come to reflect on your experience.

What to do on your placement

Make the most of every opportunity while you are there by helping out when appropriate and asking plenty of questions. This doesn't mean you should get in the way but neither should you stand back and hide in the shadows.

Remember, at the end of your placement you should request a reference to add to your UCAS application so you stand out for the right reasons. If you show willing there is every chance you may be offered further work as a healthcare assistant or be invited to return in your next holiday.

Try to experience as many different specialties as possible. If you are shadowing a consultant for a week, don't be afraid to ask them if they could arrange for you to spend some of the time with a colleague so you can experience a variety of situations.

Watch how the doctors and nurses interact with their patients and don't be afraid to chat with the patients and ask them what they think about their time in hospital. Most patients will be more than happy to chat and tell some anecdotes about their hospital experience.

Students are often asked in a medical school interview to describe a memorable patient so find out all you can about the patients and their illnesses and treatments. However, always let them know who you are and what you are doing there so you are not mistaken for a member of staff. Try to always address patients by their name and remember they are people, not just patients.

You may get the chance to talk to students or junior doctors so ask them about their course; what they find challenging and what they enjoy most.

Talk to nurses and other healthcare professionals about their role in the multi-disciplinary team and how they relate to the doctors. Ask about staff morale and whether they feel valued. It is quite likely that you will be asked in interview why you don't want to be a nurse instead of a doctor so use this opportunity to find out about their job too.

Talk to doctors about their workload and how their job impacts on their personal life as the more you understand about the whole lifestyle of being a doctor the better.

After your placement

You will probably be exhausted by the end of each day, as you will have been on your feet most of the time. However, it is really important to take time to jot some notes down in a journal or blog about what you have learnt from your experiences.

Reflection on what you have seen is a phrase you will see and hear many times as you go through the application process and it really is the most crucial part of your application, both in your personal statement and later at interview. It is not enough to simply list or reel off how many cardiograms you saw or describe complicated medical procedures. You will have time to learn those things at medical school and interviewers will only expect a basic knowledge of things you saw. Much more importantly, you need to be able to say what you felt about things you saw and it is this insight that is key to making your application successful.

You may see something that surprises or shocks you. Don't be afraid to talk to staff about what you see as they will be able to give you an insight into why it happened and what could have been done differently.

You may also see or hear things that raise ethical questions, for example discussions with patients or their families about whether or not to resuscitate them. Be prepared to discuss the dilemmas you witnessed at interview.

Observe how the health care staff communicate with their patients; by getting down to their level, explaining things in a way they understand, and asking questions to make sure they understand what is about to happen to them. Make sure you can recall some examples for interview.

Make a note of things you found difficult or challenging, like witnessing a doctor breaking bad news to a patient, or a patient with dementia attacking a nurse. Equally, try to notice the little things that make a positive difference to a patient.

Try to note down all these instances and how they made you feel or what you learnt. It will be a long time until you write your personal statement or get invited to interview and you may forget if you don't keep a record.

Chapter 4

Voluntary Work & Employment

Volunteering 35
How to organise voluntary work 37
Getting the most out of volunteering 38
Volunteering abroad 39
Fundraising & charity work 40
Paid employment 41

Volunteering

Voluntary work is probably more important for your application than shadowing, as it shows a long-term commitment and you are actually learning and applying new skills. Also, voluntary work is accessible to most people, although there may be a minimum age limit, so check this before you start. If you are particularly young, perhaps ask your teacher to write a reference for you to show that you are mature and trustworthy enough for the role you are applying for.

If you would like to volunteer in a hospital you could contact your local NHS Trust as they are often looking to recruit volunteers, either through the Trust or external organisations such as AGE UK, Hospital Radio or League of Friends. Hospital volunteers can help out in a variety of ways, for example assisting on wards, serving in a coffee shop or meeting and greeting visitors.

Other popular types of voluntary work are helping out in a hospice or nursing home. These are particularly useful as you are working in a healthcare setting alongside nurses and doctors, experiencing first-hand the physical and emotional challenges of caring for elderly or terminally ill patients. You will also gain an insight into palliative care, which is becoming more important with an increasingly ageing population and it can be especially rewarding as you are caring for people who often feel isolated.

Most hospices have a day therapy unit so there should be plenty of opportunities to assist the staff in organising social activities such as art and crafts, beauty therapy and music sessions to create a happy and friendly atmosphere. This is a good example of seeing the effects of holistic care on a patient; looking after their mental, social and spiritual well-being as well as treating their illness or pain.

Volunteering to help out at community events with St John Ambulance is a great way to learn and put into practice vital first aid skills. You will get the chance to gain first hand experience of caring for sick or injured people and improve your communication skills too by coming into contact with people from a variety of backgrounds.

If you enjoy working with children there are plenty of opportunities to volunteer with local clubs, like Beavers or Brownies, or you could offer to help out with after-school sports or craft clubs. This could give you valuable experience in explaining things in an easy-to-understand way, which is especially useful if you are interested in paediatrics or general practice later on.

Other volunteering options include working in a residential home for the elderly or in a charity shop. Of course it could be just as beneficial if you regularly help out a mother with young children or do the shopping and cleaning for an elderly or housebound neighbour.

Don't feel that you have to do something medical. There are important caring and empathy skills to be learnt in any situation where you are helping to make life easier for others.

Most of the time you will be doing the most menial tasks, such as making tea, cleaning and serving meals. You may be asked to help feed people or just sit and chat with someone.

'It's important to be adaptable; when I was volunteering at my local hospice I was asked to demonstrate Bollywood dancing! Although it may be off-putting at first, you will probably find these are some of the most rewarding things you ever do. There is nothing better than making someone smile when they see you.' – 1st year medical student

How to organise voluntary work

The longer you volunteer the better. A few weeks will not look as good as a year or more, so plan ahead. If you are doing the Duke of Edinburgh Award you will be required to do a certain amount of voluntary work over a number of months so try to combine the two.

If you want to volunteer in a hospital, hospice or care home you will probably need to have a DBS (formerly CRB) check and some basic training in health and safety before you start. You may have to wait several weeks before they will allow you to work with patients so plan this into your timetable.

Once you have found a possible setting for your voluntary work apply in person as you are more likely to get a positive response than if you write or email. Treat it like a job interview and dress smartly as first impressions count. They don't have to accept you even if you will be working for nothing.

If you are stuck for ideas, look at the following websites for up-to-date volunteering opportunities near you:

http://www.helpthehospices.org.uk/getinvolved/volunteering/

https://www.sja.org.uk/sja/young-people.aspx

http://timebank.org.uk

http://vinspired.com

http://www.do-it.org.uk

Getting the most out of volunteering

Wherever you volunteer, try to interact as much as possible with the patients and staff. Talking and, more importantly, listening to patients will not only make their day but will help to improve your communication and empathy skills. Although you may be nervous at first, it gets easier with practice and you will soon form a bond with the patients you come into contact with.

If you are not sure what to say, just smile and ask how they are and they will take it from there. Some patients may not want to chat but there are bound to be some who will welcome a friendly and listening ear.

Don't be afraid to ask the other staff or volunteers questions if you are unsure about anything, but if the members of staff are too busy, write your questions down and ask at a later quiet and more appropriate moment. Always ask what else you can do. Once you have found your feet and know your way around don't be shy to ask how you can be more involved. You will be helping them and yourself, as you'll have more to talk about at interview later.

In your application to medical school show that you have the personal attributes required for medical school, for example you are caring, have empathy skills and can work in a team, by illustrating your application with examples from your volunteering experiences.

Volunteering abroad

There are loads of fantastic opportunities for you to volunteer overseas in a medically related project. However, unless you are taking a gap year, it is likely that these will be short volunteering placements from one to several weeks and you will be asked to cover all your costs, including getting there, insurance etc.

If travel appeals to you, find out more at the following websites:

http://frontiergap.com/Volunteer/Medical-Volunteering.aspx

http://www.gapmedics.co.uk

http://www.projects-abroad.co.uk/volunteer-projects/medicine-and-healthcare

'I lived in Malawi for 5 years, and was lucky enough to witness first hand the daily challenges faced by doctors in developing countries. When water and electricity are rationed and there are not enough basic drugs available, doctors have to rely on their ingenuity and clinical skills more. The few days I spent shadowing a British doctor in a diabetes clinic in one of the country's biggest hospitals made me realise how rewarding medicine can be as a career.' – 1st year medical student.

Fundraising & charity work

Most universities are really keen to see what charitable work prospective students have done. This may include fundraising as well as raising awareness of a particular cause close to your heart. If it is something you would like to do try to choose a cause that you feel passionately about, as well as one which is medically related, so that you can easily talk about it at interview.

The smaller the charity, the greater part you can often play. Ask if you can become an ambassador for the charity and organise fundraising events where you give a presentation about what the charity does. This will help you to develop important transferable skills such as public speaking and networking.

Contact or write to people who may be interested in helping or supporting your charity, including MPs and celebrities. You never know where it might lead.

'I've been supporting Malaria No More since my brother contracted malaria. As well as raising money and completing a 'Live Below The Line' challenge, I wrote to my local MP to ask him to increase the Global Fund for malaria. To my surprise, he not only replied and passed my letter on to the Overseas Development minister, but he also invited me to give a presentation about my experiences at the House of Commons for World Malaria Day!' – 1st year medical student.

Think about setting up a Just Giving web page to help you raise funds at:

http://www.justgiving.com

Paid employment

Many students have part-time jobs to help make ends meet and this can also be a valuable part of your application if you can show that you have learnt useful transferable skills.

You don't have to be working in a medical or healthcare setting to gain skills such as communication, organisation and responsibility. Use your paid work to show you are a responsible, trustworthy and committed team member. Medical admissions personnel are always looking for students who are good team members as doctors spend a lot of time working in a multidisciplinary team.

Even a part-time job at McDonald's can be a chance to prove that you can cope under the pressure of time restraints, communicate well with customers, and are a good team player.

'I spent several months waitressing part-time in a tearoom, where I often had to deal with fussy customers. It was a great experience as I learnt to treat each customer as an individual, and to respect that they all had different tastes and needs. There was one old lady who insisted on the same teapot each time she came for tea and I soon came to understand how the little things can really make a difference to someone.' – 1st year medical student.

Don't worry if you are unable to get lots of different volunteering or work experience as not all universities will judge you negatively.

Leeds medical school says, *'In addition, applicants should possess those personal qualities which make a good doctor. These include empathy, good communication skills (speaking and listening) and a caring manner.*

The way in which you can discover whether you have these qualities, and so demonstrate them to the selectors, is by undertaking significant work experience in the caring professions. This could include voluntary or paid work in a hospital, a residential home or other caring environment. However, we recognise the difficulties faced by some candidates in arranging this type of activity and the lack of such experience does not mean that an application will automatically be rejected.'

Chapter 5

Extra-curricular Activities

Being an all-rounder 45
Getting the wow factor 47
Writing a blog 47

Being an all-rounder

Now you have sorted your work experience and voluntary work it is time to look at your personal skills and attributes and make some notes to help you with your application later.

A good doctor will have some key qualities like excellent communication skills; concern for the welfare of others; and a demonstration of being trustworthy and honest.

You can show you have these qualities by taking on a caring or supportive role at school. Be a mentor and help younger students at a maths clinic or help prevent bullying by being a school buddy. Develop your sense of social awareness by being involved in a charity event, like a sponsored run or cake sale, and demonstrate that you can take on extra responsibilities by being a school prefect or sports captain. The more you actively participate in school life the better your application will be.

Aberdeen medical school - *'Show you are an all-rounder: doctors' lives are busy and challenging but time management is very important: work hard at school; enjoy your free time to the full; demonstrate you are able to work in teams, and are able to assume different roles within the team: undertake leisure, sporting, and creative activities at school and outside school.'*

Don't forget to include any school honours or awards you have won. Maybe you took part in inter-schools maths challenges, Young Enterprise or the Young Analyst inter-schools chemistry competition, or have won sporting competitions at county or national level. If you have the opportunity to take the Duke of Edinburgh Award, then give it a go. You will gain valuable leadership and team skills, and if you manage to gain the Gold Award, it is looked on very highly.

Birmingham medical school - *'Qualifications over and above your main exams (such as the Duke of Edinburgh Award, Understanding Industry Award or General Studies) will strengthen your application by demonstrating that you have sought to develop skills that will be useful in higher education study. Although we do not normally make offers based on such qualifications, we do encourage applicants to take them and note them on their application forms.'*

If you participate in clubs or societies outside of school or have travelled overseas as part of an expedition, you should definitely mention these on your personal statement as they show you are committed and a team player. Playing a musical instrument to a high level can show commitment and motivation, but if you have played in a school ensemble or orchestra that could also be an example of being a reliable team member. Debating or public speaking shows off your communication skills, while volunteering for St John Ambulance or scouting and guiding activities all show you care for your community.

Remember to relate all your extra-curricular activities to personal qualities or attributes that the universities are looking for; don't just list them without showing what you have learnt from them.

Getting the wow factor

Almost everyone that applies to medical school will either play an instrument or a sport for their school to a high level. Try to find a unique experience or talent that will make you stand out of the crowd and your application stay out of the rejection pile.

'I was lucky enough to be invited to give a presentation at the Houses of Parliament for World Malaria Day in front of politicians and health professionals from around the world, including the head of the Global Malaria Programme for the World Health Organisation. I made sure that this stood out in my personal statement and I'm sure it helped me to be invited for interview at all of my chosen medical schools.' – 1st year medical student.

Writing a blog

A good way of reflecting on your work experience and voluntary work is to keep a diary which you can refer back to when you begin writing your personal statement and later when you prepare for your interview.

One way of doing this is to keep an online diary or blog. There are several advantages of a blog if you do it properly.

Firstly you will be regularly posting thoughts and comments about things you have seen or read or experienced in an easy-to-read format. You can choose whether to keep it private or make it public but always remember to keep your personal details confidential and never identify patients that you have seen or heard about.

By making your blog public you will be sharing what you write with a potential audience from all over the world and you may well receive comments on your posts. This will not only help you to think about the way you communicate your ideas but you will improve your written and IT skills.

You can also set up links to other like-minded blogs which you can follow as well as news feeds from health-related websites such as the BBC health news, the Guardian health website and sites such as the BMA and GMC.

Use your blog to document your achievements and work experience placements as well as to review books or health articles you have read. You can also use it to raise awareness about the particular charity you support and even link it to a fundraising page, like Just Giving.

Chapter 6

Choosing a University

University Choices...50
Teaching methods...50
Problem Based Learning (PBL)...................................51
Lecture-based courses..52
Tutorials and supervisions 52
Subject or systems based teaching.............................53
Traditional or integrated courses 54
Spiral courses..55
Intercalated degree 55
Student Selected Components 57
Anatomy...58
Elective 59
Admissions process 59
Location 61
Accommodation..62
Open Days...63
League tables 66

University Choices

Choosing a university is not easy and should definitely not be rushed. There are a limited number of universities that offer medicine, so your choice has been narrowed from the start but there are quite a few considerations to take into account. Unlike other courses you are only allowed to select four universities to study medicine. Your fifth choice must be non-medical or left empty, so the most important thing to remember is to choose wisely. Don't choose medical schools that are all highly competitive to get into, but have one or two safer options to fall back on. Try to choose universities with courses that suit your style of learning; for example, don't go for PBL courses (see below) if you don't like working independently in small groups.

Teaching methods

There are a variety of teaching methods offered by the different medical schools and it can be quite confusing if you don't understand the differences. What makes it more difficult is that many medical schools combine several types of teaching methods in varying degrees so it can be tricky to categorise their type of teaching. Fortunately they all have to cover similar material as their syllabuses are controlled by the GMC, so you just have to decide which teaching method suits you best.

There are two main styles of teaching, either the modern Problem Based Learning (PBL) or the more traditional lecture-based courses.

Problem Based Learning (PBL)

This is a relatively new style of course, which originated in Canada, and was first adopted in Britain by Manchester University in 1994. Now PBL is used by several British medical schools; including Barts, East Anglia, Edinburgh, Glasgow, Hull-York, Keele, Lancaster and Liverpool. However, this year Liverpool has decided to focus on more formalised teaching and support for students and the new course is now more an integrated spiral curriculum than pure PBL.

Students on a PBL course usually work on a given scenario in small groups with a facilitator. They start by sharing what they know about the scenario and then decide what they need to learn. Later they meet up again to discuss and evaluate their findings after which they may have to go and do further research.

The emphasis of PBL is very much on self-directed learning and you have to be incredibly self-motivated to get the most from it. The disadvantage of this style of learning is that students tend to have gaps in their knowledge because they have not had material delivered to them in a traditional way.

However it has been shown that PBL students tend to retain more knowledge compared to those students on traditional lecture based courses, presumably because they have to find it for themselves. Apparently PBL students also tend to possess better communication skills and generally work better in teams than students who followed a more traditional course.

Lecture-based courses

Most medical schools use lecture-based teaching to some extent. Course material is delivered in large lecture halls to the whole year group. The advantage of this is that all students receive exactly the same material, which makes it easier when revising for exams. However it can be impersonal and may not give students the opportunity to discuss the material easily.

Tutorials and supervisions

Oxford and Cambridge use the traditional lecture format to teach most of their material. However, both also uniquely offer either tutorials (at Oxford) or supervisions (at Cambridge).

Due to the specialist environment, with the high ratio of tutors to students, these are often one to one sessions and they can take place up to 4 times a week. During these sessions students cover material in much more detail so they can acquire a much deeper understanding of the subject.

However they can be incredibly intense and require a huge commitment, which often only suits certain students.

Subject or systems based teaching

Subject-based Teaching is delivered through individual subjects such as anatomy, biochemistry, genetics, pharmacology, pathology and physiology. These courses are less common now and tend to be taught at more traditional medical schools that use a lecture-based course.

Systems-based Teaching looks at different systems in the body, such as the digestive system, cardiovascular system, endocrine system, respiratory system, and musculoskeletal system. Each system is looked at in turn and students learn all of the anatomy, physiology, pharmacology, pathology, biochemistry, genetics and clinical skills relevant to that system.

The main advantage of this method of learning is that the subjects become more relevant compared to learning them in isolation and it can help to motivate students as they can see why a subject is important. However, the disadvantage is that each system is looked at in isolation and it can be hard for students to spot links between them.

Medical schools using systems based teaching include Aberdeen, Barts, Dundee, Durham, East Anglia, Edinburgh, Leicester and Liverpool.

Traditional or integrated courses

Traditionally, medical students spend the first 2 or 3 years learning the basic medical science and then go out on clinical practice. However, it is more common now to have an integrated course, which means there will be some clinical practice taught alongside the basic medical sciences and vice versa. Many medical schools offer early patient contact to motivate their students.

Traditional courses may appeal to you if you want to acquire the theoretical scientific knowledge before having clinical contact with patients. However, there are criticisms that students are out of touch with real medicine. Aberdeen, Cambridge, Imperial and Oxford all offer traditional courses.

Integrated courses are courses where the basic medical sciences are taught together with clinical studies. This means that you will have some early clinical contact in your pre-clinical years and later when you are on clinical practice you will also have lectures or PBL. Integrated courses encourage the application of evidence-based learning as you are applying your knowledge in a real context and you get a holistic view of the patient. They are popular with students who want to get as much patient contact as early as possible.

However, the disadvantage is that students don't understand all the theory before they treat patients and fundamental scientific theories may be left out altogether.

Most medical schools offer integrated courses, including Aberdeen, Cardiff, Dundee, Durham, East Anglia, Edinburgh, Glasgow, Hull York, Keele, Leicester, Liverpool, Newcastle and Nottingham.

Spiral courses

Some medical schools teach using a spiral curriculum which, as the name suggests, means that topics are revisited on several occasions at different points in the course, each time with a more clinical focus and increasing depth. First the relevant scientific foundations are taught before the pathological and clinical aspects of that topic are developed further.

Universities, which teach using this spiral approach, include Barts, Dundee, Durham, Edinburgh, Glasgow, Keele, Kings and Leeds.

Intercalated degree

An intercalated degree gives students the opportunity to gain a further BSc or BA degree during their medical course.

It takes different formats at different universities but usually takes one year after either your second or third year, making the total length of the course six years instead of five.

Students can choose from subjects like biochemistry, anatomy, physiology or pharmacology, or choose medically related topics like ethics, medical law or history of Medicine.

Some universities offer all their students the option to take an extra degree between their second and third year in medical school. However, others only offer the highest achieving students the chance to intercalate; while universities like Cambridge, Oxford and UCL include an intercalated degree as a compulsory part of their course so you need to choose where you apply carefully.

Nottingham University offers the unique chance to intercalate during the five-year course without having to study for a further year.

An intercalated degree gives you the chance to study a particular subject in depth and may involve a substantial amount of research. It can also be useful for your future CV to set you apart from other junior doctors when you apply for specialties.

However, some students can't afford to do one or don't want to waste time doing one if they can start earning earlier especially if they have taken a longer route to get to medical school. It is therefore important to consider whether intercalating appeals to you now as it could affect your choice of university.

Student Selected Components

Student Selected Components (SSCs) are projects or short courses in medical, scientific and non-medical subjects, which allow students to direct their own learning and to widen and increase their knowledge. There may be possibilities to take a range of SSCs throughout the course or just at specific times.

Subjects available to study vary between universities but may include topics like modern languages, care of the elderly, social and psychological studies, or palliative medicine. They may also be based around clinical scenarios, patient interviews, history taking and associated issues surrounding a chosen patient.

Most medical schools offer some sort of SSC in their curriculum but you will need to visit their websites for specific information.

Anatomy

Most medical schools tend to offer prosection instead of the more traditional dissection.

Prosection is where an experienced anatomist dissects the cadaver and students are presented with a particular part to study whereas with dissection the students do it themselves.

There are advantages to both approaches and unless you feel strongly about one particular approach it probably won't be a huge factor in your choice of medical school. More schools have moved towards prosection as they believe the students get a better experience of anatomy this way. However, if you are a very practical person you may prefer to do the dissection yourself.

Other ways of teaching anatomy that are becoming more popular include self-directed learning and computer-assisted learning.

Medical schools offering dissection include Aberdeen, Cambridge, Dundee, Keele, Nottingham, and Sheffield. King's offers both prosection and dissection.

Elective

Most medical schools offer the opportunity for students to take an elective at some point in the course. Most electives last between 4 and 8 weeks and take place near the end of the course. Students can choose to take their elective in a specialist service in the UK or overseas, either in a developing country such as Malawi or Tanzania, or in a modern hospital like California.

Most students find their electives educational and rewarding and gain invaluable clinical experience in a very different environment and culture from their own.

Admissions process

Most medical schools require an admissions test before offering a place; either the UKCAT or BMAT and most of them will also interview applicants, with just a couple of exceptions, such as Belfast and Edinburgh.

The other medical schools will either interview in a traditional way with a panel of interviewers who will ask questions for about 15 or 20 minutes or they will carry out group interviews or multiple mini interviews (MMIs) which can be quite intensive and last up to an hour.

MMIs are being used increasingly more by medical schools including Birmingham, Dundee, Lancaster, Leeds and Manchester. Sheffield and Liverpool, however, are known for having quite laid-back, friendly interviews, which are meant to make the candidate feel as relaxed as possible.

Most medical schools will require you to achieve at least 3 A grades in your GCE A levels although there are a few who might ask for slightly higher grades like Birmingham who ask for A*AA or Cambridge who ask for A*A*A.

The admissions process should definitely be a factor to consider when narrowing down your choice of university. Try to choose universities with admissions procedures that suit your abilities best. If you are better at exams than interviews opt for medical schools that rely more on outstanding results. However, if you are better at communicating face to face than sitting exams, choose medical schools that don't focus so much on the test result before they interview.

Another thing to take into account is the size of the year and ratio of applicants to number of offers. Some medical schools are smaller than others, for example Durham, Keele and Exeter take between 100 and 130 students each year compared to larger intakes of around 370 by Manchester and Liverpool. Some medical schools have a much larger number of applications each year than others, for example Leeds and Liverpool with over 4,000 applications each.

'Learning facilities, academic support and the availability of pastoral care may also influence your choice of university, as well as availability of specialist sports, clubs and societies, so do your research thoroughly and don't leave anything to chance.

Location

The location of the university can be a very important factor when choosing where to study. You may want to move as far away from home as possible or you may have dependents that you have to be near. However, try not to narrow your options too much as you really need to take other factors into consideration when choosing a medical school and play to your strengths. If you are happy to live far from home that's fine but bear in mind that there may be times when you need to go home unexpectedly or you may become ill and need collecting, so work out the costs involved in travelling long distances.

There are pros and cons of living in both a large city or a smaller one and you will need to consider living costs, price of eating out, rental accommodation, cost of transport etc. London is probably the most expensive place to live with other cities in the south costing considerably more than northern cities.

You may also feel strongly about either living on a campus or living in the middle of the city. All the London medical schools are city based with the exception of Barts, which is set on a campus.

Some medical schools share campuses and you may have to move from one site to another during your time studying, for example if you choose Durham, you may be placed at the Stockton-on-Tees campus for 2 years and then move to Newcastle-upon-Tyne. The best advice is to visit some of your choices and see for yourself. Don't listen to what other people or friends think, make up your own mind.

Other factors for consideration include whether you would prefer to live near the sea for sailing or surfing activities or inland for hill walking. Find out about the nightlife and shopping facilities if that is important to you. Remember, you will have to spend 5 or 6 years or more in the same place. Most graduate medical students end up working in the vicinity of their medical school so it is a pretty long-term decision you are making.

Accommodation

Accommodation may also be important to you. Generally most students are guaranteed a place in university halls for their first year. The standard, type and cost of accommodation can vary significantly, however, within each university and between universities.

You have to consider whether you want to self-cater or live in catered halls and whether you want a room with a shared bathroom or an en-suite shower.

You may want to check out how far away the accommodation is from the medical school; it may be just a few minutes walk or a bus ride across the city.

Some university accommodation has not been updated since it was built so it may be looking pretty shabby whereas other accommodation might be spanking new with hi-tech gadgets. Try to find out if Wi-Fi is available in your room and if laundry facilities are nearby.

Many universities have virtual tours of their campus and accommodation available on their websites so check these out when making your choices.

Open Days

Towards the end of the summer term most universities hold Open Days for prospective students to look around the campus and departments that they are interested in. Even if you are not sure if you want to study medicine at this stage, it is useful to attend a few Open Days at a few of your favourite universities as they can give you some valuable information about the admissions process and you can also get a feel for the ethos of the school.

June and July are also pleasant months to go touring and the universities look their best in the sunshine.

It is best to research the different medical schools and choose at least 5 or 6 to visit, so that you can discard a couple that you don't like and still have 4 to apply to.

Once you have narrowed down your choices, visit each medical school's website and search for their open days.

Most universities have 2 or 3 different dates available, either at the weekend or mid-week. Plan a timetable that allows to you to fit in as many as possible but check that you can have time off school if you choose mid-week days. Schools generally allow students to take off a couple of days for visits but may not allow more than that.

You will often need to book a space on an Open Day if you want to be sure of attending all the relevant sessions about the course. Some are on a first-come first-served basis, so do make sure you book in plenty of time. Although the Open Days usually start in June, you can register for a place as early as March so try to book a few before Easter.

The most valuable sessions are the ones that explain the selection process. Here you will find out the latest up-to-date information about entry requirements; how they use admissions tests like the UKCAT or BMAT and what they are looking for in personal statements.

Take a notebook with you and write everything down, as after a few open days you will forget who said what. Another handy tip is to take a tablet or iPad with you and photograph the presentations to look at again at your leisure.

Make the most of the opportunities to chat with admissions tutors, medical students and other prospective students as you will get a feel for the place from what they say.

Also make time to look around the whole campus, including the accommodation, as this may sway your decision one way or another. Don't forget to wear comfortable shoes and take a waterproof jacket, as much of the day you will be walking long distances and there may be hills involved, for example in Bristol.

If you are planning to travel to the university by train, it's a good idea to get yourself a student rail card and book trains in advance to avoid high fares on the day. Most students take a friend or parent with them, however they may not be allowed into certain talks with you, especially if the course is popular as priority is given to prospective students.

Aberdeen Medical School - *'The appeal of chosen institutions may well be confirmed or dismissed by the student who has spent some time exploring the Medical School site and facilities, and questioning staff and undergraduate students.*

Choose your schools for positive reasons, having found out as much about different schools' curricula, facilities, patient availability, location etc. as possible. You may be asked to justify your choice at interview. Your research should include use of university websites, prospectuses and leaflets; discussions with medical students and doctors.'

League tables

There are quite a few different university league tables and you will find that universities can be near the top of one and yet near the bottom of another.

There are a few universities that always hold the top positions and which are world famous, like Oxford and Cambridge, but generally medical schools are all pretty similar. They all have to teach the same syllabus decided by the General Medical Council and they generally only differ in teaching style.

Most medical graduates will leave university and be guaranteed a job, so there is very little to distinguish the medical schools. If, however, you want to find out more, look at the websites below for the latest information.

http://www.theguardian.com/education/table/2013/jun/04/university-guide-medicine1

http://www.thecompleteuniversityguide.co.uk/league-tables/rankings?s=medicine

Chapter 7

Admissions Tests

Why you need to take a test 68
The BMAT 70
What is in the BMAT 71
How the BMAT is scored 72
How universities use the BMAT 73
Practice questions & suggested reading 74
The UKCAT 75
UKCAT preparation 76
The UKCAT format 76
Verbal reasoning 77
Quantitative reasoning 78
Abstract reasoning 80
Decision analysis 81
Situational judgement 81
Useful UKCAT resources 82
Booking your UKCAT 84
The day of the test 85
Taking the test 86
Getting your result 87
How universities use the UKCAT 88

Why you need to take a test

Most medical schools use an admissions test to help them identify the best candidates. As so many applicants are predicted top grades, it helps the admissions staff to have an unbiased and fair test to compare candidates. There are two tests that are used and they both test the ability of students to think critically under pressure.

It is likely that you will have to take at least one clinical aptitude test before you apply to study medicine and because they are not cheap it might be best if you choose universities that all require the same test.

As Birmingham, Bristol, Liverpool and Lancaster medical schools are the only ones that don't require applicants to take an admissions test at present, you will be very limited if you opt only for those and you will not necessarily be taking the easiest option. It is highly likely that many applicants will put at least one of these choices as a safety net in case they don't do as well as they hoped in the admissions test so there is likely to be more competition. Also, although they don't use the clinical aptitude tests, Birmingham, for example, have very high academic requirements and a tough MMI interview process which tests many of the same attributes as the other aptitude tests so don't think that it is an easy option to get into.

Most of the medical schools require applicants to take the UKCAT test before applying which tests skills rather than knowledge.

However, if you apply to Brighton and Sussex, Cambridge, Imperial College London, Leeds, Oxford or UCL you will need to take the BMAT, which is a more science based test.

The advantage of the UKCAT over the BMAT is that you can take it and have the result back before you apply to medical schools so if you don't do as well as expected in it you can apply to those universities which have a lower cut-off or weight it lower. With the BMAT, you take the test and get the result after you have chosen your medical schools so if you do badly it is too late to change your options.

Unfortunately you can't retake the test during the same cycle if you don't do well; you will have to wait until the next year to do so. However, the best option is to practise as many questions and simulation mocks so you know what to expect in the real test.

If you are in Year 11 now you may want to try taking a trial test this summer. You will have to pay and you won't be able to use your result for your UCAS application as UCAS only accept test results taken in the year of application.

However, having experience of the test environment and the test format will give you an advantage over others taking the test with you the following year, as it will take away some of the anxiety from an unknown situation.

It is widely acknowledged that students who perform poorly the first time significantly increase their score second time around. Most students don't have that luxury, however, as the test is not only expensive but most students don't plan their application that far ahead.

The BMAT

The Bio-Medical Admissions Test (BMAT) is a subject-specific admissions test and is compulsory for students applying for medicine to Brighton and Sussex, Cambridge, Imperial College London, Leeds, Oxford and UCL. It is taken in early November for admission the following October. You will need to book your test before October 15th and testing starts from November 5th, with results released online on November 26th. You have until December 5th to query your result if it is not as good as you expected.

The test is 2 hours long and consists of 3 sections. Candidates are allowed to use a soft pencil and rubber for Sections 1 and 2, and a black ink pen for Section 3. Tippex, dictionaries and calculators are not allowed.

The test doesn't need a lot of extra study as it is a test of skills and knowledge that students are expected to have already. However, it is definitely necessary to revise your old GCSE maths and science topics and also to be confident in your A level maths and science subjects.

The BMAT costs £44.00 for a standard entry fee (or £75.50 for a late entry) in the UK and EU. It costs £74.00 for a standard entry fee (or £105.50 for a late entry) in the rest of the world.

You can take the test at any centre that administers the BMAT and you must register with the test centre. If you are still at school, your school or college may be able to administer the BMAT for you. However, if you are not at school or college, you will need to find a centre where you can sit the test, by going to the website below.

http://www.admissionstestingservice.org/find-a-centre/

What is in the BMAT

The BMAT is divided into three sections: Aptitude and Skills; Scientific Knowledge and Applications; and the Writing Task.

Aptitude and Skills: this section tests skills in problem solving, understanding arguments, data analysis and inference. It comprises critical thinking type questions, focusing on your reasoning skills and your ability to think concisely and logically under a time pressure. It is 60 minutes long and comprises 35 multiple choice and short answer questions.

Scientific Knowledge and Applications: this section tests the ability to apply scientific knowledge from school science and mathematics (up to and including the National Curriculum for England Key Stage 4) and includes questions on GCSE level maths, physics, biology and chemistry. It is 30 minutes long and comprises 27 multiple choice and short answer questions.

Writing Task: this section tests the ability to select, develop and organise ideas, and to communicate them in writing concisely and effectively. There is one essay question from a choice of four and they are usually based on an ethical, philosophical or debatable topic of Medicine. It is 30 minutes long and the essay must not exceed 550 words on one sheet of A4, although you are given space on the question paper for making notes.

How the BMAT is scored

The test is scored with questions in Sections 1 and 2 worth 1 mark each. The total raw marks for each section are converted to the BMAT scale, from 1 (low) to 9 (high). Typical BMAT candidates will score around 5.0. The best candidates will score around 6.0, and a few exceptional candidates will score higher than 7.0.

The essay in Section 3 is marked by two examiners. Each examiner gives 2 scores – one for quality of content (on a scale of 0–5), and one for quality of written English (on the scale A, C, E).

The 2 scores for Section 3 are combined and if the two marks for content are the same or no more than one mark apart, the candidate gets the average of the two marks. If the two marks for written English are the same or no more than one mark apart, the scores are combined like this: AA = A, AC = B, CC = C, CE = D and EE = E.

So, an essay given a 4C by one examiner and 4A by the other will get a final score of 4B. An essay given 3C by one examiner and 2C by the other will receive a mark of 2.5C. If there is a larger discrepancy in the marks the essays are marked for a third time and the final mark is checked by the Senior Assessment Manager.

The test is designed to highlight the most able students so expect it to be a lot more difficult than most other exams you have taken and don't be upset if you don't think you've done very well as most people taking the test will find it difficult.

How universities use the BMAT

Brighton and Sussex – *'The results of the BMAT will be used to assess each application and will form part of the process to select applicants for interview. BMAT may also be used as a final discriminator if needed after interview.'*

UCL – *'The BMAT scores are used, along with other information in the UCAS application, to help us select candidates for interview.'*

Leeds School of Medicine will be using BMAT ns process for all applicants applying in the ... cycle. We do not intend to operate a "cut-off threshold" below which we would not consider an application; instead we intend to use performance in individual test sections to help us assess applicants with "non-traditional" educational backgrounds. In future, for "traditional" applicants, we will take it into account alongside previous and predicted academic performance, personal statements and references.'

Practice questions & suggested reading

You can download practice BMAT questions at the website below:

http://www.admissionstestingservice.org/help-me-find/resources/specimen-papers/

The following books have been recommended by the admissions testing service to help students prepare for the thinking skills required for the BMAT.

- *Thinking Skills* by John Butterworth and Geoff Thwaites
- *Critical Reasoning: A Practical Introduction* by Anne Thomson
- *Critical Thinking: A Concise Guide* by Gary Kemp & Tracy Bowell
- *Critical Thinking for Students* by Roy Van Den Brink-Budgen

- *Thinking from A to Z* by Nigel Warburton
- *Critical Thinking: An Introduction* by Alec Fisher
- *The Logic of Real Arguments* by Alec Fisher

The UKCAT

The UKCAT test is a clinical aptitude test designed to test how well students can think under pressure and how they would react in certain situations. It is designed to be a fair test so as not to discriminate against students from better schools. It's not an exam that measures student achievement and it doesn't contain any curriculum or science content.

The following universities currently require the UKCAT: Aberdeen, Cardiff, Dundee, Durham, East Anglia, Edinburgh, Exeter, Glasgow, Hull York, Imperial College (graduate entry only), Keele, King's College, Leicester, Manchester, Newcastle, Nottingham, Plymouth, Queen Mary London, Queen's Belfast, Sheffield, Southampton, St Andrew's, St George's London and Warwick (graduate entry only), but check the website of your chosen university to confirm their entry criteria as they can change at any time.

UKCAT preparation

Many people will tell you that you can't revise or prepare for the test but this is not true. Make sure you spend several weeks in the run-up to your test preparing and practising so that you can achieve your best possible score.

There are plenty of practice questions available online and in books, but it is really important to practice under timed conditions as this is the only way to improve your score. The UKCAT result is almost always one of the first criteria that universities look at when deciding who to short-list for interview and they may well discard your application based on your score without even looking at your predicted grades or personal statement.

The UKCAT format

The test is made up of five sections: verbal reasoning, qualitative reasoning, abstract reasoning, decision analysis and situational judgement. The biggest difficulty is not the level of questions but the time available to answer all the questions. However, you are not penalised for giving a wrong answer, so make sure you complete every single answer as you will have a 1 in 4 chance of getting them right even if you just guess (or a higher chance if you can eliminate 1 or 2 answers based on common sense).

Verbal reasoning

The verbal reasoning section is made up of 11 passages of text, each followed by 4 questions relating to what you have read.

There are several different types of question, some of which are statements followed by the options: True, False, or Can't Tell. Other questions ask you to make inferences or draw conclusions from the information given and others require you to complete a statement or question with the best response out of a choice of 4.

All of the questions will require you to quickly scan the text and answer the question on the basis of the information in the passage. You must not use your own knowledge of the subject and you don't have to learn anything for this test.

The best preparation is to practice answering as many questions as you can under timed conditions. You only have 2 minutes to answer each set of 4 questions, which is not very long at all.

It is probably best to spend a minute reading the text and then 15 seconds answering each question. However, you will not be able to keep up this speed for all 11 passages, so if the answer is not obvious then make a sensible guess and move on quickly.

The best way to practice is to use the free online questions but you can also practice by reading articles on news websites as quickly as you can and then try to reflect on what you have read. If you read health-related articles this will also help you to prepare for your interview later. Do not be disillusioned if you take too long answering the questions at first; it will get easier. Try to concentrate fully by sitting in a quiet room without any distractions. Turn your phone and music off and clear your work surface of any clutter that will distract you. Concentration is key to answering these questions.

Quantitative reasoning

The quantitative reasoning section comprises 10 sections, each with 4 questions followed by 5 options to answer. You will have about 2 minutes to answer each set of 4 questions and will need to take information from either a graph, chart or table.

The maths is of a level similar to GCSE level and mostly includes questions involving percentage changes, areas and volumes, times and timetables, conversions and ratios. This is a section that you can revise for.

As you probably know, Maths at A level is very different to that at GCSE and so you may be a little rusty. Go back to your old textbooks and go over the arithmetic topics before trying some of the free online questions.

The trick here is to read the question first and then pick out what information you need from all the information you are given. It is likely that you won't need to use all the information that is given. At the same time make sure you scan everything on the page. There may be some crucial information hidden in the small print.

Make sure you check the units given as you may have to convert units before you start your calculation. Usually at least one question just requires you to look at a graph and make a choice without doing any calculation at all. Make sure you allow yourself time to get these easy points. If you look at a question and don't like it, then guess, flag it for review and move on. The easiest questions are not necessarily at the start.

The on-line calculator is quite awkward to use and you should practice using it before the day of your test. You can try it out on the UKCAT website's practice questions. It only performs very basic calculations and is not nearly as good as your own scientific calculator. If there is a number pad on your keyboard, then use it to input data. This is much quicker than using the mouse and cursor and will save you valuable seconds. Jot answers down on the whiteboard provided as you may need to refer back to them for later questions and this could also save you valuable time.

Abstract reasoning

The Abstract Reasoning section tests your ability to infer relationships between sets of objects. There will be two sets of shapes labelled A and B and you will be asked to put test shapes into either set A, set B or neither set, based on a rule that you have to work out.

You will probably find that this section looks the most difficult when you first take a look at the UKCAT and it will take a while for you to work out what it is all about. However, with a lot of practice, you will soon find that you start to spot patterns more easily and begin to recognise repeating concepts to look out for.

With 65 questions to answer in only 15 minutes it seems like an impossible task but you will find that your speed dramatically increases with practice. There are 13 pairs of sets with 5 test shapes to assign to one of the sets or neither. Once you have identified the pattern it will only take a matter of seconds to categorise the test shapes so spend the majority of the time working out the pattern.

If you can't see the pattern after about 45 seconds then guess, flag the question for review and move on. Like the last section, you will often find easier questions towards the end of the section.

Decision analysis

The Decision Analysis section is probably the section that most students find the easiest. Put simply, it is code deciphering and it uses logic and judgement to select the best response. There are only 26 questions and there is more than enough time to complete this section. However, there are often a couple of answers which are very similar and you have to look at each piece of information very carefully so you don't fall in the trap of choosing the wrong one. It may be useful to write the codes down on the whiteboard if you feel you can afford the time so you don't get too confused.

Situational judgement

This section is relatively new and although tested and marked last year, the results were not taken into account by the universities. This year, however, it will be assessed and it is designed to test a candidate's empathy, integrity and team working ability in different ethical scenarios. You have 26 minutes to answer 71 questions associated with 17 scenarios. There will be between 3 and 6 response options based either on how appropriate something is or how important and responses should relate to what an individual should do, rather than what they may be likely to do.

Full marks are awarded if your response matches the correct answer and partial marks awarded if your response is close to the correct answer.

With practice, it is fairly easy to use common sense to get to the right answer or close to it and at the end you will be assigned a level from 1 to 4, with band 1 being the highest.

Candidates scoring a band 1 have performed exceptionally and well above average, showing similar judgement in most cases to the panel of experts, whereas candidates scoring band 4 have performed low with judgement differing significantly from ideal responses to questions in many cases.

Useful UKCAT resources

The official UKCAT survey suggested that use of books relevant to the UKCAT was associated with higher overall test performance, as they can contain helpful strategies and additional practice questions.

However there is also lots of free advice available on the web as well as many sources of free practice questions and, unless the book has been published very recently, it is unlikely to include the correct test content and timings and new test items.

http://www.ukcat.ac.uk/preparation

I recommend buying at least one book to help you as you'll need to practice with as many questions as possible.

Get Into Medical School 600 UKCAT Practice Questions by ISC Medical is a great resource especially for the Abstract Reasoning and Decision Analysis questions. However, the Quantitative Reasoning questions are much harder than the actual UKCAT questions and can be off-putting. Also the Verbal reasoning questions are probably out-dated now as the UKCAT have changed their format and tend to ask very few questions like the ones this book offers. Try to find the most recent publication.

http://www.amazon.co.uk/into-Medical-School-comprehensive-explanations/dp/1905812094

Score Higher On The UKCAT by KAPLAN is also a great resource and this copy has been updated for the new type test.

http://www.amazon.co.uk/Score-Higher-UKCAT-questions-Medicine/dp/0198704313/ref=sr_1_2?s=books&ie=UTF8&qid=1393587577&sr=1-2&keywords=score+higher+on+the+ukcat+kaplan

There are also plenty of courses available that will claim to help you succeed in the UKCAT test. However, these can be expensive and may not be all they claim to be so try to get a personal recommendation before splashing out on one. The official UKCAT survey did not conclude that applicants' scores were raised significantly by going on such courses, but you must make up your own mind.

Booking your UKCAT

You can register for the test any time from 1st May and testing begins on 1st July until 3rd October. However, registration ends on 19 September so don't leave it too late to register. You can choose any time and day that you want to sit the test, between July and October, but the earlier you book the test the more choice you will have available to you. Try to pick a day in the holidays when you will be more relaxed and not stressed with school and homework. The cost of the test increases the later you take it so bear this in mind too.

Think about the time you pick carefully. Are you better in the morning or do you prefer to lie in and work better in the afternoon? Try to practise at home at the same time as you have picked for your test so that your brain gets used to your routine and it doesn't have a shock on the day!

There is an extended version of the UKCAT called the UKCATSEN for people with special needs so make sure you apply for this if it's relevant to you.

The test is held at official Pearson VUE centres around the country and internationally although there are some countries that do not have test centres and are exempt from taking the test. Allow yourself plenty of time to reach the centre which is most likely situated in your nearest town or city. If you are planning to travel there by train you might want to book it after the peak travel times to save yourself some money.

The day of the test

Plan your journey carefully with an alternative route ready just in case. The test centres are also used for other tests, for example driving theory tests so there will be a variety of people attending the same session as you and if you arrive late you may be refused another time slot.

The UKCAT is two hours long so make sure you have eaten a good breakfast beforehand so you are not distracted by your tummy rumbling. A bowl of porridge or cereal is probably best as it will slowly release energy throughout the test to help you keep going. Lay off the tea and coffee though as you will not be able to pause the test once it has started to go to the loo! If you do need to go to the toilet, the test will keep running and you will lose vital time so make sure you have been in advance. Timing is the most important thing on the test so try not to waste it.

Remember that this test is going to kick-start your medical career so use your adrenalin to your advantage. If you are too laid back then you will find it hard to react quickly enough to answer the questions in time.

However, if you find your nerves are getting the better of you, make sure you are well organised and have a bag packed with all the documents you need the night before.

Arrive at the test centre in plenty of time and then go and have a walk nearby for ten minutes to distract yourself. Take plenty of deep slow breaths and imagine yourself coming out of the test with your certificate having done well.

Taking the test

You will take the test in a small cubicle, sitting at a desk with a computer and you should be given the choice to wear headphones to prevent distractions from other people taking their driving theory or other tests. Make sure you are comfortable before the test starts as you don't want to waste time adjusting your seat.

You are not allowed to eat or drink once you are in the test area so make sure you have had some water before you start (but not too much in case you need the loo!)

You will be given a laminated sheet of A4 paper with a whiteboard marker pen before you start. Make sure your pen works and ask for a spare one if they let you, as you may have to wait for them to replace it during the test and they might not notice that you have put your hand up to get their attention especially if they are particularly busy.

Take a few deep breaths before you start to relax and settle your nerves.

Some computers do not display the whole page on their screen so you may have to scroll down to see the bottom of the page even if you have already answered the question, as you will not be allowed to move on to the next page if you haven't done so. This can be very frustrating and may waste precious time.

It is advisable to use the keypad to type in numbers onto the on-screen calculator, instead of moving the cursor to the numbers as this saves time.

The on-screen calculator is very small and has barely any functions on it, so you can't save answers and it can be frustrating if you haven't practised using it before. However, you can avoid frustration on the day by practising on the online tests which are available on the UKCAT website.

http://www.ukcat.ac.uk/preparation

Getting your result

You will receive your score as soon as complete your test. It will be between 300 and 900 – the average score being 600. It is almost impossible to predict what score you will get from the practice questions you do, so don't even try. However, if you have practiced a wide of range of questions, you should hopefully be pleasantly surprised when you get your score.

It will be tempting to rush to the social media sites to compare your score with other hopeful medical students, but beware of this. The students that post results on these sites are just a tiny sample of all the students who will be sitting the test. Also, students are more likely to post their results if they are exceptionally good so the statistics that appear on these forums may be biased.

Remember the UKCAT is only part of the whole application process so don't beat yourself up if you haven't done as well as you hoped. You still have a very high chance of getting into medical school if you apply strategically. A few medical schools don't use the UKCAT test at all and others have lower cut-off points than others, so do your research and do not waste a choice by applying to a university with a high cut-off however much you want to go there. It is better to get into one school than none!

If you have performed exceptionally well, congratulate yourself but don't become complacent. You still have to impress admissions tutors with your academic grades and personal statement.

How universities use the UKCAT

There are three main ways that medical schools use the UKCAT.

A few medical schools use the UKCAT score as a tiebreaker where a decision has to be made between two very similar candidates, or to offer interviews to candidates that score very highly on the UKCAT but perform poorly in other areas of their application.

Other medical schools weight the UKCAT score with other scores from predicted or actual grades, personal statement, reference etc. and use it as a factor in whether to make an offer of an interview or the offer of a place.

Lastly, some universities have a cut-off threshold for the UKCAT score below which the applicant is rejected and above which it is used to decide whether or not to offer an interview. This is used by the majority of medical schools, where the thresholds vary from using average scores across the subtests, to looking at the lowest scoring subtest so it is important to score well in every subtest.

Look at the quotes below about how 3 different universities use the UKCAT score:

'All applicants must score 2500 or above in the UKCAT exam in order for their application to be considered further. The Faculty of Medicine will then be ranking applicants by UKCAT score and a certain percentage will be invited to attend a selection day.' - Southampton University

'It is likely that any candidate with a score of 2600 or above will be given consideration.' – Sheffield University

'We look at the individual components of the UKCAT and mark them along with the applicant's personal statement, answers to our online questionnaire and their GCSE results.'
– University of Nottingham.

At first glance at the information given, it appears that Southampton has a lower cut-off than Sheffield. However this is not strictly true. Although Southampton University's cut-off score is lower than Sheffield's, once they have rejected anyone with a score below the cut-off of 2500, they will then rank everyone's score and only pick the top 50% or so to invite to interview. This means that a score of 2600 will pass the cut-off but may fall below the percentage necessary to be chosen for interview. However, if you have a score of 2600, Sheffield University will consider your application on a level pegging with other applicants who have scored much higher than you and the UKCAT score will no longer be used in the selection process.

Although Nottingham does not specify a cut-off, your score will be used along with other criteria so if you feel you have a strong personal statement and high GCSE grades it may be worth a gamble applying even if your UKCAT score is relatively low.

See the most recent ways that universities use the UKCAT results in Appendix 3. If in doubt, phone the admissions office and ask to talk to someone about it. They may not publicise the information but they can be very helpful if you ask.

Chapter 8

Your UCAS Application

UCAS 92
Your personal statement 93
Start early 95
Make it personal 95
The first draft 96
Edit 99
Submit it early 101
Your school reference 102

UCAS

UCAS is the Universities and Colleges Admissions Service and you have to apply to medical school through them by completing an online UCAS application.

http://www.ucas.com

Your UCAS application consists of your personal statement and your school reference as well as your grades and predicted grades. You do not need to send in your admission test results as they are sent to UCAS automatically.

On your application there will be space to apply to 5 universities. However, you are only allowed to apply for 4 medical schools and the remaining space can either be used to apply for a non-medical course or it can be left blank.

You can opt to defer entry to university for a year, but you need to check with individual medical schools first to make sure that they will accept a deferred entry. Don't forget that the application process is incredibly competitive and there will always be a certain number of students who will not receive any offers in one particular admissions cycle, so bear this in mind when thinking about deferring entry as you may not get in first time and end up deferring for two years instead.

Don't forget that the deadline for applying to medical schools (and Oxbridge) is earlier than for other non-medical courses so don't be caught out. It is usually 15th October but check this to be sure.

Once you register on UCAS you will receive a unique ID number, username and password which you will need to keep safe. You will also need to pay online for the privilege of using the service.

You can now follow your progress on UCAS Track where you will receive notifications that the universities are processing your application, inviting you to interview, offering you a place on a course, or rejecting your application. UCAS Track will always email you with a notification of any changes to your application so you do not need to constantly check it, however sometimes the notification can take a day or two to come through especially in busy times like the end of March.

Your personal statement

This is a 4,000 character or 47 line statement about why you want to study medicine and what work experience you have done to help you make that decision, as well as the other qualities and attributes you have that would make you a good doctor and an asset to your chosen medical schools.

It will be marked by the admissions staff at each of your chosen medical schools according to a set of criteria and the score you receive will be added to other marks taken from your reference, predicted and actual grades and admission test results so it is really important that it ticks all the right boxes.

However each medical school has their own set of criteria and want applicants to demonstrate different skill sets so it is important to check the advice each of your chosen schools offers and then write your statement to the highest standard set so it meets every school's requirements. For example, look at the advice from Manchester University below:

'Make your personal statement original, interesting and enthusiastic. Use varied sentence structure, make it relevant, and apply for the course not the career. Don't just talk about how you want to be a doctor, mention why you want to study medicine, your love of science etc. Follow the ABC – Activity, Benefit, Course.

For example,
Activity – a part-time job serving customers in a shop
Benefit – learnt responsibility, communication skills and how to manage time well
Course – relate it back to the course you want to study, for example, "I will find it easy to manage the workload on the course and to relate to patients." '

Start early

Your UCAS form needs to be sent off by mid-October in the year before you want to go to university (usually year 13). Don't leave it until the last minute! By thinking about it for at least 6 months before it is due, you will notice any gaps in your achievements and experiences and you will have time to fill these with necessary work experience, voluntary work etc.

It will take a lot longer to write and perfect than you imagine! Try to have at least the first few drafts written by the end of the summer holiday before you go into year 13 so that you have plenty of time to work on it without the added pressure of school and homework. Believe it or not, by the time you are ready to submit it in October, you will probably have changed it many, many times, hopefully for the better.

Make it personal

The clue here is in the name. Make sure it is all about you! It is very easy to write in general terms, but you really have to make sure every word is directly about you and your experiences and relate these to the best attributes of a doctor.

You only have 4,000 characters to use so you need to be really succinct and leave out any unnecessary words.

This is not the place to waffle or use overly complex vocabulary. You are not writing a novel so throw away your thesaurus and let your voice be heard.

Don't be tempted to make anything up or exaggerate the truth at all. Doctors must be honest and trustworthy at all times and if you are found out, that could be the end of your medical dreams. It will be put through a plagiarism test after you have submitted it so don't take any risks.

The first draft

When you first sit down to write it, let the words flow. Start with a blank sheet of paper and brainstorm.

Think about all aspects of yourself, not just the academic side or your interest in medicine. You need to show that you are well rounded and have a variety of interests.

Ask yourself the following questions:

What do you enjoy doing? Why?
What work experience have you done? What did you learn from it?
What made you want to be a doctor?
What are the drawbacks you've seen or heard about?
What voluntary work have you done? How have you changed as a person during this?
How do you relax?

What sports do you play? At what level?
What have you done that will make you stand out from the crowd and how can you make it relevant to medicine?

When you have brainstormed and have a list of all your achievements and experiences, you can begin your first draft. Try to show evidence of your commitment to Medicine through your work experience and give examples that show you have the core qualities required of a doctor. You also need a unique selling point if possible. What have you done that will make you leap out from the thousands of other applications?

Your personal statement should read like a journey with a beginning, middle and an end. Start with why you want to study medicine and your hopes for your career, followed by what you have done to prove that medicine is right for you and finally finish with a description of your extracurricular activities and hobbies that show that you are right for medicine and will be an asset to the university.

The hardest part of your statement is usually the very first sentence so leave that out and start from the second paragraph. You can come back to the start once the rest is written, by which time you may have a strong sentence in the middle that you can pull out and use as an introduction or a quote that ties in nicely with the rest of your statement.

Perhaps you have had a unique personal experience or have done something unusual that will surprise the reader so mention it early on to grab their attention, but try not to shock them or it may backfire on you.

However you start, it must be punchy and stick in the reader's mind or your hard work is likely to end up in the reject pile. An example of a weak introduction is something like, 'I want to do medicine because my granddad was in hospital once with...' This doesn't show why you should be a doctor, just that you might be good in a caring profession like nursing.

Equally, don't write so that you come across as arrogant or boastful. 'I would make a great doctor because....' is not going to make the reader warm to you. However you do have to sell yourself and you can do this by describing what attributes you have using examples of extra-curricular activities. For example you can show you are a good team player with leadership skills by describing a group activity you started or led.

You can show your commitment by writing about your work experience, but avoid mentioning specific hospitals or doctors by name, however eminent they may be. Rather than just list all the work experience that you have done, it is better if you can show what you have learned about a medical career and its implications. Talk about a patient you met and how their treatment affected them as this is an excellent way to show your empathy for their condition.

If you weren't able to organise a medical placement, then be sure to mention an interesting article you have read but be prepared to talk about the subject matter in depth at interview.

Whatever you do, try to make the statement read in an engaging way. You need to write in a formal style but at the same time make yourself attractive to the reader and try to let your enthusiasm and motivation shine through.

Your last sentence must be just as strong as the first as this is the last impression the admissions tutor will have of you before they decide whether or not to invite you for an interview. Try to tie it in with your opening paragraph, without repeating yourself, so the statement is cohesive.

Edit

Once you have completed your first draft you will need to edit your work to make it the best you can possibly make it and so that it fits the required character limit. While you are editing your statement you can check how many characters or lines you have used by going to this handy website and pasting in your personal statement. It is a lot quicker and easier than using the UCAS site.

http://maccery.com/ps/

You need to write in a formal style of English avoiding colloquialisms or abbreviations. For example, instead of *I'm* write *I am* and write *cannot* instead of *can't*.

Avoid repeating the same word in different forms, for example *fascinated, fascinating, fascination* especially if they are close together in the statement.

Try not to use connectives like *and, also, however*; instead write in concise sentences and edit constantly by removing any unnecessary words. Every word you write should have value and be there for a purpose.

Don't waste space with unnecessary detail. You don't need to put exact dates of work experience in or name doctors or hospitals. You also don't need to talk about your academic qualifications; your grades will speak for themselves and are already in your application elsewhere.

Ask plenty of people to proof-read it before you submit it, as however many times you read it, there will always certainly be one or two spelling or grammatical mistakes that your eye misses.

Try to get the help of someone who knows about writing personal statements to check that it is the best it can be, but beware of allowing them to re-write parts for you as the admissions tutors will soon pick up on an older voice. It must sound like you!

It is useful to ask a teacher or family member for advice, but do not show your statement to friends or fellow students who are also applying to university as there is a chance that they might, consciously or subconsciously, plagiarise your work and it could jeopardise your own statement. UCAS uses software to detect any evidence of plagiarism and, if detected, the application will be withdrawn from the selection process.

There are plenty of personal statements available online which may give you an idea of the standard required. Be aware though that not all statements posted online are good ones. Try to read them critically and decide if you think they deserve a place at medical school.

Look at the websites below for examples:

http://medblog.medlink-uk.net/medschoolpersonalstatements/

http://www.thestudentroom.co.uk/wiki/category:medicine_personal_statements

Submit it early

Submit your personal statement as early as possible and don't leave it to the night before the deadline. Remember doctors need to be good time managers and well organised so it looks better if you get it in early.

Many admissions staff will look at it as soon as you submit it and may well ask you for an interview before the deadline, especially if they don't have to wait for UKCAT or BMAT test results. As the number of interviews is limited an early submission could really stand in your favour.

However, don't worry if you don't hear anything until the following year as many of the medical school admissions are notoriously slow at responding due to the high number of applications they receive.

Your school reference

You may think that you can't do anything about your school reference but you must ensure that you are given the best reference possible as some medical schools will score it and combine the score with other scores for your personal statement, extracurricular activities etc.

It is not rocket science to realise that in order to get a good reference you must work hard at school all year and achieve top grades in all your tests. However, it is also important that the right teacher writes your reference and that he knows and likes you well. If you are assigned a teacher for your UCAS application process that you do not get on with, you should ask another teacher if you can swap, as a poor reference could make the difference between getting an interview or not.

If you are happy with your choice of referee, you must make sure that they are aware of why you want to study medicine and how much it means to you. Also let them know in plenty of time about any extra-curricular activities you do both in and out of school, what positions of responsibility you hold at school and any prizes or achievements you have earned.

It is also a good idea to give them references from people whom you have worked for, doctors you have shadowed or from voluntary work you have undertaken. Do not assume that they will ask you for these, but make sure that they have them as they will help the teacher to get a more rounded picture of you both at school and in other contexts.

Make sure that your predicted grades are good enough to get you through the selection process for your chosen medical school. If you have applied to medical schools that want an A*, then your referee must predict an A* and not an A. If they won't predict a high enough grade then change your choice of medical school or you will be wasting a choice.

To give you an idea of what your teacher may be asked to write, look below at some of the guidelines put together to help with the writing of a reference for someone applying to the Edinburgh Medical School:

• *Include predicted grades in the predicted grades section of the UCAS form. An application cannot be processed without these.*

- *Show evidence that the applicant, as well as being excellent at science, is also a well-rounded person.*
- *What is the applicant like as a person? Do they have integrity, are they honest, and responsible, do they show empathy?*
- *How does the applicant get on with peers and teachers? Would they make a good leader? Do they have good interpersonal and organisational skills? Are they able to work as part of a team?*
- *What activities are they involved in at school – sport, music or other clubs and hobbies? Do they help out with students in other years?*
- *Confirm what you can of the applicant's personal statement regarding extra curricular activities.*
- *Through career exploration the applicant should discover early on that medicine is not just about science but also about communicating with people. It is vital that the applicant understands this and this is why we attach so much importance to work experience.*
- *Don't repeat how well an applicant has done by giving a summary of exam results.*
- *Give clear confirmation of any circumstances which might have led to a poorer result than expected in the exams.*
- *Has the applicant overcome educational or social disadvantage?*

Don't be afraid to ask your referee if you can see the reference before they send it off so that you can ask them to amend anything that you feel is unfair. If they refuse and say that it is confidential, just thank them and leave it.

'My teacher predicted that I would get 3 A grades because she thought that if she predicted A*s then the universities might ask for A*s, and it would be too much pressure for me. However, one of my choices always gave offers including at least one A*, and I was afraid that I wouldn't meet their entry criteria with predicted grades of 3As. She agreed to amend the predicted grades to include an A* and luckily I received an offer from the medical school for A*AA.' – 1st year medical student.

Chapter 9

Important Background Knowledge

Know your facts 107
NHS 107
GMC 109
Tomorrow's Doctors 110
BMA 111
NICE 111
The Francis report 112

Know your facts

Before your interview you should make sure you are up to date with important medical and health-related topics and have some understanding and knowledge of relevant medical organisations. Although you will learn more about these at medical school, you should have done enough research to show that you are aware of issues that affect everyone and that you know something about the profession that you are applying for. Treat it like any other job interview and make sure you know your facts.

Below are a selection of some of the most important organisations and topics that you may be asked about with links to their websites to find out more. The more you read about them and discuss issues with medics, friends, parents or teachers, the better an understanding you will have.

Keep up to date with the news as you will be expected to know the very latest, such as the Ebola crisis, obesity, diabetes and the problems of an ageing population.

NHS

The NHS (National Health Service) was introduced in 1948 by health secretary Aneurin Bevan, to provide good healthcare and services free of charge to all at the point of delivery.

For the first time, all hospitals, doctors, nurses, dentists etc. were brought together under one umbrella organisation financed entirely from taxation which meant that people paid into it according to their means.

It is now the world's largest publicly funded health service and is the envy of other nations. However, although it was initially thought that better access to healthcare would result in better health for everyone and eventually costs would be lowered, the opposite has resulted. More people are living longer and more expensive new treatments are available so rationing has to be applied.

Today the NHS is undergoing major changes in its structure including who makes decisions about NHS services, service commissioning and the way money is spent.

The Health and Social Care Act took effect in 2013, and brought in the most wide-ranging reforms of the NHS since it was founded in 1948.

'It puts clinicians at the centre of commissioning services, frees up providers to innovate, empowers patients, and gives a new focus to public health.' – NHS

Locally, clinical commissioning groups, made up of doctors, nurses and other health professionals, buy services for patients, while local councils promote public health.

An updated NHS Constitution was published in 2013 to improve: patient involvement; feedback; duty of candour; end of life care; integrated care; complaints; patient information; staff rights, responsibilities and commitments; dignity, respect and compassion.

Find out more about the recent changes to the NHS below:

http://www.nhs.uk/

GMC

The GMC (General Medical Council) regulates doctors and ensures good medical practice. It has issued a document called Good Medical Practice that sets out the standards expected from registered doctors.

http://www.gmc-uk.org/guidance/good_medical_practice.asp

The GMC also makes sure that medical schools, not only equip students with the scientific knowledge and technical skills they need to be a doctor, but also enable them to commit to high personal and professional values. It sets standards for teaching, learning and assessment and it has issued a document called Tomorrow's Doctors for medical students which sets out the knowledge, skills and behaviours that medical students must learn at UK medical schools and be able to demonstrate.

The duties of a doctor registered with the GMC are summarised below.

- Doctors must show respect for human lives and make the care of their patient their first concern.
- They must promote the health of patients and the public and provide a good standard of care, including keeping their knowledge and skills up to date.
- They must treat patients politely and with consideration, and respect their right to confidentiality as individuals.
- Doctors must work in partnership with patients, listening and responding to their concerns, and giving them the information they need in a way that they understand, to help them make their own decisions with respect to their treatment.
- They should be honest and open and always act with integrity and without discrimination towards patients or colleagues.
- They should report without delay anything they see or know which they believe puts the patient or public at risk, so that the public's trust in the profession is upheld.
- Doctors are personally accountable and must be prepared to always justify their decisions and actions.

You can read more about Tomorrow's Doctors by clicking on the link below:

http://www.gmc-uk.org/TomorrowsDoctors_2009.pdf_39260971.pdf

BMA

The BMA (British Medical Association) represent doctors locally and nationally. They are the medical profession's trade union and professional body, and they negotiate with the government over pay and working conditions. They are committed to ensuring all doctors are treated equally and they handle employment issues and offer confidential advice and counselling for both doctors and medical students.

http://bma.org.uk

NICE

NICE (National Institute for Health and Clinical Excellence) was set up for the NHS, local authorities, charities and other organisations that commission or provide health care, public health or social care services.

NICE supports healthcare professionals to make sure that their care is the best quality and the best value for money and it provides independent and evidence-based guidance on the most effective ways to prevent, diagnose and treat disease and ill health, reducing inequalities and variation. There are often ethical dilemmas over the fairness of availability of resources and it is the role of NICE to make recommendations to the government based on evidence of effectiveness of treatments and their cost.

http://www.nice.org.uk

The Francis report

Following an extensive inquiry into failings at the Mid-Staffs NHS Foundation Trust, Robert Francis QC published his final report on February 6 2013. It highlighted a whole system failure, not just one NHS trust. There weren't enough checks in place that were working adequately to ensure patients were treated with dignity and didn't suffer harm. The report made 290 recommendations, including a more patient-centred approach, better medical training and nursing, better complaints handling, service governance and regulation.

There is an excellent timeline of events with links to each story as it was reported on this BBC news website:

http://www.bbc.co.uk/news/uk-england-stoke-staffordshire-20965469

Chapter 10

Ethics

Ethical dilemmas 114
Autonomy and competence 115
Beneficence 116
Non-maleficence 117
Justice 117
Confidentiality 117

Ethical dilemmas

Ethics questions are very common in interviews and you will need to understand and explain the 4 pillars of ethics to be able to discuss the different ethical dilemmas.

Some common ethical issues are arguments for and against euthanasia and abortion; the dilemma whether to respect the choice of a Jehova's Witness to refuse a blood transfusion against the need to do the best for a patient; and issues regarding who should receive a transplant.

It is essential that you always argue both sides of the argument and don't show too much of a strong opinion in case you appear arrogant. Always look at the dilemma from the point of view of everyone involved, including the doctor, the patient and the patient's family or dependents. Also discuss what effect the outcome will have on society as a whole.

Could the decision lead to a slippery slope effect? This means that if we allow something relatively harmless today, we may start a trend that results in something currently unthinkable becoming accepted.

Try to come to a balanced conclusion, but be prepared for the interviewers to argue your choice.

Remember that there is never one correct answer with these types of questions and the interviewers are more interested in how you reach your conclusion than what it is. If there were correct answers then they would not be dilemmas!

Autonomy and competence

The first pillar is autonomy which means that the patients are responsible for deciding their own care. As a doctor you have a responsibility to make sure that your patient understands all the relevant information to be able to make an informed decision about their treatment.

You also have to consider whether or not your patients might be influenced by other people such as family members who may pressure them into a certain decision.

Another issue that doctors have to assess which comes under the pillar of autonomy, is whether or not the patient is competent. If they are under 18, then you will have to determine whether they are 'Gillick' competent.

Mrs Gillick took her local health authority to court to prevent them supplying contraceptives to children under 16 without parental knowledge or consent.

However, Lord Fraser ruled that if a child fully understood the risks of the treatment and its implications, that they were competent and had autonomy to make their own choices and had the right to confidentiality.

This became known as 'Gillick' competent and applies to all medical situations. If the patient is not 'Gillick' competent however, you would have to involve their parents in their care. If a patient is not competent, or is unconscious and not able to decide on their own treatment, then as a doctor you must act in the best interests of the patient taking into account a living will and the family's views.

Beneficence

The second pillar is beneficence, which means doing good and always acting in the best interest of the patient. This does not necessarily mean doing what the patient wants however and sometimes the doctor will face a dilemma between what is in the patient's best interest and the autonomy of choice that a patient has.

Non-maleficence

The third pillar is non-maleficence, which means not harming the patient. This can be tricky because a course of treatment may hurt the patient or cause side effects, but if the benefits outweigh the risks, then it may be the best course of action. It can also lead to dilemmas for a doctor.

Justice

The fourth pillar means treating all patients fairly and equally and making sure that all patients have access to the same treatments regardless of where they live. The National Institute for Health and Clinical Excellence (NICE) is responsible for overseeing the fair distribution of resources.

Confidentiality

This is not a pillar but is important in its own right, as a patient has the right to confidentiality, except in exceptional circumstances, for example if their illness poses a risk to others. To find out more about ethical issues, go to:

http://bma.org.uk/practical-support-at-work/ethics/medical-students-ethics-tool-kit

http://www.bbc.co.uk/ethics/euthanasia/

Chapter 11

Preparing for an Interview

Why you will be interviewed 119
Waiting 120
Preparation 121
Background reading 121
Interview questions 124
The most commonly asked questions 126
Practising 130
Structuring your answers 131
Being positive & selling yourself 132
Using your personal statement 132
Answering the question 133

Why you will be interviewed

Once the admissions staff have checked academic and non-academic criteria, that is your predicted and actual grades, admissions test result and personal statement, they will still have too many applicants for places. The interview process is important for them to assess what sort of doctor you will make. However good you look on paper, if you have trouble communicating or appear arrogant at interview you are unlikely to make it to medical school.

Although there is no stereotypical doctor, the admissions staff are looking for certain attributes and qualities that a good doctor should have. You can find these yourself by going to the GMC's website and looking at Tomorrow's Doctors, which sets out the qualities of a good doctor.

http://www.gmc-uk.org/education/undergraduate/tomorrows_doctors.asp

Each medical school will place a different emphasis on different criteria, but in general, they are all looking for signs of motivation and understanding; empathy and integrity; good communication skills and evidence of a good team player.

Waiting

Once you have submitted your UCAS application, you just have to be patient and wait. Hopefully you will receive an invitation to interview (there are only a few medical schools that give out offers without an interview), but this may take weeks or months.

Meanwhile, your friends who have applied for other courses and who submitted their UCAS applications much later than you, will start to get offers for places rolling in. Don't despair; it may not be fair but it is perfectly normal. Medical schools can be very slow to contact you and tend to send out invitations to interview in dribs and drabs. They may even make a few applicants a conditional offer before you have even heard from them, but this doesn't mean that your application is worth any less than theirs. It is just how the system works.

Make sure you check your email account regularly, especially your spam account as many messages from universities are treated as spam and will be deleted automatically after a few weeks if unnoticed. Sometimes invitations to interview are sent by email, other times they are sent by post, or they may be posted on your UCAS track first, so check all of these regularly.

Social forums like the student room often have stalking pages set up where students can notify others whenever they receive invitations to interview, offers or rejections for each university.

This can be useful for you to identify key times when universities are contacting hopeful students, but it can also be soul destroying if you see others receiving news while you hear nothing.

Don't despair though; the medical schools are under so much pressure that it can take a long time for them to notify everyone. Remember, in this case no news is definitely good news! Despite what people may think, the order in which people are notified has no bearing on anything. It really is completely random due to the huge number of applicants they have to process. It is not done alphabetically, or preferentially.

Preparation

Start preparing for your interview as soon as you have completed your UCAS form. Don't wait until you receive an invitation to interview. You usually only get a couple of weeks' notice, and you will need to be up-to-date with current health news, have prepared and practiced your answers to the predictable questions and have an understanding of medical ethical dilemmas as well as knowledge of how the NHS functions.

Background reading

Try to read at least a couple of health-related news articles every day.

If you have been keeping an online diary, then this will be easy to manage. Set up a few RSS news feeds directly to your blog or website. Try the Guardian health news and the BBC health news sections as these are free to read and have links to similar articles.

http://www.theguardian.com/society/health

http://www.bbc.co.uk/news/health/

If you prefer to read the Times, New Scientist or the Student BMJ, you will need to subscribe to read their full articles. However, if you spot an interesting headline in these journals, then search for the story on-line and you may find it on another free website.

http://www.thetimes.co.uk/tto/health/

http://www.newscientist.com/section/health

Don't just read the articles; if you find an article that is of particular interest to you, jot a few lines about it in your blog with a link to the original article. Don't write copious notes about it as you will just waste time.

If you bookmark it or put a link to the article, you will easily be able to access it again in the future and swot up on the subject just before your interview. This is just like cutting out a newspaper article and sticking it in a scrapbook, only less messy!

Try to read a variety of health articles, including articles about the NHS, political issues, ethical articles and the latest medical advancements, to ensure that you can talk about a range of issues at interview. The best types of articles are those that describe ethical dilemmas, as they are interesting to talk about in an interview and have no right or wrong answers. Political issues can be controversial in an interview, depending on the political stance of your interviewer, so try to avoid discussing these if you can.

Don't worry if you don't understand all the medical terms you read about in scientific journals, you will learn those at medical school. The admissions tutors are looking for people who are caring and compassionate with an enthusiasm for medicine, not fully-fledged medics. However, you should have a general knowledge of the most common illnesses, like diabetes, coronary disease etc. and have heard of the latest medical breakthroughs like stem cell research.

Check out BBC iplayer for radio podcasts and television programmes, which often have interesting health-related articles.

http://www.bbc.co.uk/podcasts/radio4/genre/factual/healthandwellbeing

The NHS website also has a handy roundup of news on its website.

http://www.nhs.uk/news/Pages/NewsIndex.aspx

...w questions

If you want to access hundreds of typical medical interview questions for free, then you can't do better than looking at the ISC website below.

http://www.medical-interviews.co.uk/interview-questions-medical-school-interviews.aspx

However, I recommend investing in their medical interview book, 'Medical School Interviews' by Olivier Picard and George Lee, which has all the questions together with model answers. This is a great resource but make sure that you purchase or borrow it in plenty of time to use it to its maximum. It is easy to browse through, but if you are serious about preparing then try to work through the questions methodically.

Read each question and brainstorm your own answers before reading their model answer. When you have read the model answer and come up with your own take on it, using your own experiences and observations, then jot some notes down on a postcard, so you gradually build up your own library of model answers.

These will be easy to swot up on just before your interview and you will know that they are not only effective answers but also unique to yourself. But careful you don't just learn the model answers as everyone will be trotting out the same answers and you'll just end up sounding like everyone else.

There are some questions that are definitely bound to come up in some form or other. The most obvious one is 'why do you want to study medicine?' or 'why do you want to be a doctor?'

Make sure you have a well-rehearsed answer but don't learn it parrot fashion as this will come across to the interviewer and you need to sound original and spontaneous. Instead have a few well thought out reasons with personal examples that you can confidently articulate.

Be prepared to come up with reasons for your answer in case the interviewer challenges you but don't be put off. There is often no right or wrong answer as long as you can give valid reasons for your choice. If you say you want to study medicine for the money though you may be disappointed that you don't receive an offer. Try to sound caring and compassionate in your answer, remember this is a vocational degree.

Many interviewers will want to know that you are aware of the challenges of medicine and are not going into it with rose-tinted glasses. You may be asked how you would deal with stress, what makes you angry, how you relax, how you have dealt with failure. Answer honestly but try to show the interviewer that you will be able to cope and have strategies in place to combat stress, angry patients, failure etc. Talking about a variety of coping mechanisms, such as playing sport or a musical instrument or prioritizing tasks, will show you are a well-balanced student.

Working as part of a team and being able to lead a team are essential requirements of the job, so be prepared for questions about times you have both been a useful team member and led a team yourself. Have plenty of examples so you don't end up repeating yourself. Being a school captain, participating in Duke of Edinburgh awards and being part of a sports team are useful experiences. Make sure you have those types of experiences now or else get started quickly.

Ethical dilemmas are a real favourite so that interviewers can judge how you would deal with a situation. Remember not to leap to a conclusion without first discussing the issues involved, keeping in mind the 4 pillars of ethics; autonomy, beneficence, non-maleficence and justice. Also examine the argument through the points of view of all the people involved, particularly the patient, but also the patient's family, the doctor, the cost to the NHS etc.

The most commonly asked questions

The questions on the next page are all actual questions asked in recent interviews and they come up over and over again so make sure you have prepared answers or at least thought about how you would answer them.

Questions just to help you relax (not meant to trick you):

- How are you?
- How did you get here today?
- How was your journey?
- Have you come here on your own?

Questions about your motivation:

- Why do you want to study medicine?
- When did you first decide to study medicine?
- Tell us about your work experience.
- What challenges do you think a career in medicine will pose to you? How will you deal with them?
- Have you talked to medical students or junior doctors? What did you learn?

Questions about your knowledge of being a doctor:

- What are the pros and cons of being a doctor?
- How will you cope with the cons?
- What do doctors do apart from treating patients?
- What is a multi-disciplinary team? Who is part of it?
- Why not nursing or another caring healthcare profession?
- Tell us about something medically related which you read about recently.

Questions about the medical school and its course:

- Why do you want to study here?
- What attracts you the most about our medical school?
- What methods of teaching do we use here?
- What do you know about PBL? How does it compare with other learning styles? What are the advantages or disadvantages?
- How do you go about researching something you know nothing about?
- What clubs or societies would you like to join if you came here?
- Why should we offer you a place here?

Questions about your personal attributes:

- How did your communication skills make a difference to a situation?
- Are you a leader or a follower?
- Give an example where you played an effective role as a team member.
- What are the attributes of a good team leader?
- Tell me about your leadership skills.
- How do you manage your time?
- How good are your organizational skills?
- How would you deal with a big personality?
- What are your hobbies?
- How do you reduce stress?
- How do you cope with stress?
- What are your main strengths?

- What attributes do you have that would make you a good doctor?
- Tell us about an achievement of which you are proud.
- What are two of your main weaknesses?
- Describe a time when you were disappointed.
- Describe the biggest challenge you have ever faced.
- How would your friends describe you?
- If you could change one thing about yourself, what would it be?
- How do you cope with criticism?
- How will you manage the large amount of independent study?
- What makes you think you can cope with the long stressful process of studying medicine?
- What are the advantages and disadvantages of admitting when mistakes are made?

Ethical Questions:

- You are a junior doctor and just before the morning ward round you notice that your consultant smells of alcohol. What do you do?
- One of your patients finds out they have AIDS, but refuses to tell their partner. What do you do?
- Another student on your course suddenly starts missing lectures and acting out of character. What would you do?

- In your exam you notice a student is cheating. What do you do?
- What do you think is the biggest problem faced by the NHS today, and how could it be improved?

Practising

The average medical applicant spends 40 hours preparing for interview. Practise all the time, whenever you have a spare moment - in the bath, on the bus to school and before you go to bed, until you are clear in your mind exactly why you want to be a doctor, study medicine, go to a particular university. However hard you try, you probably won't be able to come up with an original answer but make it personal to you and your experiences.

When you feel you are ready, practise in a formal environment with an 'interviewer' or panel of 'interviewers', as this is the best way to get used to the interview process and find weaknesses in your answers or the way you deliver them. Teachers or professional friends or neighbours can be useful 'interviewers' and it is probably best not to ask your parents if you want to keep it 'professional'.

If you can bear it, film yourself during the mock interview and you will be able to play it back and look out for any nervous tics or bad habits that you might need to work on.

You'll be amazed at how often you repeat something like, 'you know what I mean?' or drum your fingers on the edge of the table. Try to get as much feedback as possible afterwards, ask your interviewers to be brutally honest.

There are several interview preparation courses available which are useful if you are worried about the process but they can be expensive. There are also excellent resources available online for free including this video by Kevin Ahern, an American medical school lecturer.

https://www.youtube.com/watch?v=OLxz4pCBXKo

Structuring your answers

Try to limit your answers to 1-2 minutes. Stopping yourself from talking when you are nervous can be really difficult, however interviewers are likely to lose concentration after a couple of minutes of hearing you talk.

Structure your answers into 3 or 4 main points to make it easy for interviewers to follow and stop yourself from waffling. Most structured points can be given within 1-2 minutes, leaving time for further questions.

For ethical or decision-making questions, make sure you always talk through what you are thinking. There is often no right or wrong answer but the interviewers want to see you logically discussing both sides of the argument or problem.

Being positive & selling yourself

Interviewers want to hear how great you are and it is important that you are not shy when telling them about your achievements and why they should choose you. All the candidates will be selling themselves so you must too. Turn everything into a positive. Even if they ask about your weaknesses, you should tell them what you have done to overcome them.

Using your personal statement

Your personal statement should be structured to say why you want to do medicine, what work experience you have done and what interests you have and these are three of the most commonly asked questions. Make sure that you talk about all the best points that you have written down and don't assume that the interviewers have read it beforehand.

Tell your story. Saying generic things like 'I'm a good team player' will not score you as many points as using personal experiences and reflecting on what you have learned.

Answering the question

Make sure you understand what has been asked and get straight to the point without giving a long introduction.

If you don't hear the question, don't be afraid to ask them to repeat it for you.

Interactive stations will often provide you with written information either before or upon entering the station. Try to stay calm and read the instructions or scenario carefully. Mentally highlight the important points and make sure you understand what they want you to do before you start.

Chapter 12

The Actual Interview

Getting an interview..135
The night before your interview.........................135
The morning of the interview...........................136
When you get there...137
Body language...139
Appearing confident..141
Multiple Mini Interviews (MMIs)............................143

Getting an Interview

At last your UCAS track page has changed and one of your medical school choices has invited you for an interview. You have received an email from the university telling you when and where the interview is and what you need to take with you. When you have finished celebrating, make sure you reply to the admissions staff, accepting their invitation and thanking them. If, for some reason, you cannot make it to the interview on that particular day, you should phone the admissions team and ask if they can reschedule it. However, this should only be in exceptional circumstances as you do not want to jeopardise your chances.

The night before your interview

You may have chosen to stay in the university's city prior to your interview or you may be travelling up on the day. Whatever you have chosen to do ensure that you have your clothes prepared and ironed, shoes cleaned and know where and when you need to be at the interview location.

Boys should wear a suit, whereas girls have a bit more choice. Most girls wear either a trouser suit, skirt and jacket, or dress and jacket. It may be very cold so wear a smart cardigan or jumper that can be removed if it is warm in the building.

Girls' shoes tend to vary from flats to heels and boots, but whatever you choose to wear, make sure they are clean. It is more important to feel comfortable than glamorous as you may have to trek round the university on a tour. In fact it may be worth taking two pairs of shoes to avoid blisters.

Read over your personal statement several times so that you know it inside out and can answer any questions about it and check your interview letter again. Make sure you know exactly where you need to go and when you need to register as this may be a few hours before your actual interview.

Then try to relax and ensure you have an early night and a good sleep. Now is not the time to go out on the town or watch a late-night film. Set the alarm so that you wake up in plenty of time to get dressed, have breakfast (you don't want your tummy to rumble during the interview!) and prepare yourself.

The morning of the interview

Dress smartly, with minimal jewellery or accessories. You are not there to make a fashion statement; instead dress to make yourself appear older than you are. You have to come across as a potential doctor not a trendy student.

Tie long hair back so that you don't have to keep flicking it out of your eyes in the interview. Wear sensible shoes as you may have to walk a long way if you are taken on a tour of the university. Also take a bottle of water with you as it is likely that you will get a dry mouth after talking for a length of time.

Allow plenty of time to travel to the interview in case there are traffic problems or trains are delayed. Most interviews take place during the winter months so there may be snow, storms or flooding which can affect both train and road travel.

Make sure you have directions and a phone number with you in case you need to contact the university admissions staff to let them know you are delayed. However, do everything possible to arrive early and have a walk before you go into the medical school to clear any cobwebs and settle your nerves.

When you get there

When you arrive at the venue you will probably need to register first so that the organisers know that you have arrived. This is the time to hand over any documents you've been asked to bring, like ID and GCSE or A level certificates. There may be refreshments provided and you will be told where you can wait prior to the interview.

An interviewer will usually call you in once they are ready. It's a good idea to talk to someone before you go in, whether it's a medical student or another applicant waiting to be interviewed, as it will help you to relax and make sure your voice isn't wobbly.

'Before one of my interviews there were some medical students who I chatted to. They were really friendly and put me at ease by giving me advice and telling me about the city and the course, which came in useful during my interview.' – 1st year medical student.

Some applicants like to take a friend or parent with them, which is fine, although one is probably enough, as too many people with you can be distracting. Don't bring your granddad and great-aunt for a day out as this may appear a little odd.

Check out the waiting area to see if other parents are waiting there. If not, politely ask your parent to leave you and tell them you will call them when you are finished. Remind them not to call you though in case your phone goes off in the middle of the interview. It is probably best to switch it off at this point before you forget.

Before you go in remove your outdoor coat and leave it with someone in the waiting area. It is advisable to leave any large bags there too so that you are not overloaded, in case you appear clumsy or awkward.

All you should take in is a bottle of water, which you should put down when you are in the room and don't forget to close the door behind you when you go in the room.

Body language

Your unconscious body language is incredibly important and can play a vital role in effective communication. However, it can be difficult to know how to sit, who to look at or what to do with your hands during an interview.

When you first meet the interviewers, try to make the first move and greet them by shaking hands firmly. This immediately shows them that you are confident and also that you are their equal. Remember they are looking to recruit a future doctor and they need to see you as a potential doctor not a child.

If they introduce themselves by their first name, use it as they will be treating you as an equal and you should do the same.

Sit down and lean slightly forward with your feet firmly on the floor and your hands crossed and forearms resting on your thighs. In this position you will look calm and ready and you should be able to keep the position comfortably for the whole interview.

In between questions you can sit back slightly, but try not to lean too far back as you will look as if you don't care and equally don't lean too far forward as it can appear intimidating. Don't cross your arms, as this can convey hostility.

Don't forget to smile! Smiling conveys confidence and will generally make you appear more attractive to the interviewers. It is also contagious and you may find that the interviewers smile back and appear less intimidating.

Remember they are looking for a highly motivated applicant and so it is important that show enthusiasm and passion for the subjects you are discussing however nervous you may feel inside.

Make eye contact with the interviewers from the start. If you find this difficult, then focus on their eyebrows when you talk to them as they will think you are looking at their eyes. If there is more than one interviewer in the room, it can be tricky to know who to look at, so make sure you look at the person who is talking to you and nod politely to show them that you are listening.

When you are answering questions, try to make eye contact with all the interviewers and not just the one who asked the question. At least one of the interviewers will probably be looking down making notes so don't worry about keeping eye contact with them.

Appearing confident

Remind yourself that you have been shortlisted for this interview. That means you have beaten hundreds of other applicants to get there, because your personal statement and academic achievements stood out. So have confidence in yourself!

Your voice will give you away if you are nervous. Try to practise speaking from the bottom of your stomach so that you don't sound squeaky and high-pitched. Be aware of how fast or slowly you talk. You don't want to garble, but don't put the interviewers to sleep either. Vary your pitch and dynamics to sound more interesting and generally try to match the volume of your speech to that of your interviewer.

Don't forget to pause for a breath at appropriate moments. Take a few moments to organise your thoughts in your head. Keep to the point and try to explain things clearly. An answer should not take longer than about 1 to 2 minutes, as any longer and the interviewer will lose interest and you will be in danger of waffling.

Use the appropriate jargon if you know it. Remember you are trying to come across as a doctor, not a school child. However, if you don't understand a question or acronym, say so. The interviewers should reframe the question, giving you extra time to think of an answer.

Never be afraid to say you don't know something, it is a sign of a good doctor if you can admit the truth - tell them if you haven't covered the topic at school and they will hopefully move on.

Always try to give positive, upbeat answers that convey your enthusiasm and illustrate your answers with specific examples from your work experience. Tell your story, so that they remember you and you don't just blend in with all the others. This is your time to shine, so sell yourself.

Towards the end, the interviewers usually ask if you have any questions for them. It's a good chance for you to find out more information about the medical school, but don't ask anything obvious that you could have found out by looking at their prospectus or website.

If you don't have any questions, then that's fine, you can always ask them when you are likely to hear back about the interview. At the end of the interview, don't forget to thank them for their time. Last impressions count as much as first.

'Some tips for your interview are: relax, prepare well, say what you think, be familiar with the course, be honest, don't exaggerate, don't ramble on, and don't fabricate.' - Student Recruitment Officer, Nottingham University.

Multiple Mini Interviews (MMIs)

MMIs are a type of interview format that is growing in popularity. They have been compared with speed dating, as instead of a traditional panel interview, the candidates have a series of shorter interviews with different interviewers and each interview is usually marked on its own merit.

This can be an advantage as you have a clean start at each interview, but it can also be incredibly demanding and intense and you don't have time to build a rapport with any particular interviewer, which can be frustrating. However, if you perform badly at one interview it will not affect any of the other interviews.

Your individual scores from each interview station are usually added together and an average taken and you often have to reach at least a minimum standard in every interview to be offered a place.

These types of interviews usually include a variety of interview techniques, such as role-play, ethical scenarios and practical or group tasks which may suit students who are uncomfortable with a more formal type of interview. They are designed to test the candidate's communication and team working skills, problem solving and decision-making skills, motivation, compassion and empathy in different situations. Sometimes the interviewers may be actors who have been primed how to react; but more commonly they are medical students or doctors.

Medical schools that currently use MMI are Aberdeen, Birmingham, Bristol, Dundee, East Anglia, Hull York, Keele, Lancaster, Leeds, Leicester, Manchester, Queens Belfast and St George's, but more and more are changing to this format so it is important to be prepared for some form of MMI type interview.

Some examples of actual MMIs are given below:

At Birmingham, there are six separate interviews, lasting six minutes each. Interview stations are designed to assess aspects such as motivation for medicine; communication; self-insight; ethical reasoning; data interpretation; ability to evaluate information and identify relevant aspects. Recently, the six stations included:

- motivation and insight into Medicine through discussion of specific aspects of your work experience; in particular, those experiences that allowed you to observe the management of patients by professional healthcare workers.

- dealing with personal and ethical challenges through thinking about your own experiences and an ethical problem, you should demonstrate personal qualities important for coping in a demanding career.

- interactive task where you need to show how comfortable and confident you are meeting a new person, and having a short conversation with them covering issues of substance. The qualities that the task measures includes listening, questioning, engaging and responding appropriately to what another person says.

- debate task where you will be expected to identify the issues that are of particular relevance to a healthcare topic and, through discussion of these, highlight why this topic is subject to debate. You should also present your arguments for possible courses of action.

- ethics task where you should demonstrate your ability to consider and communicate about ethical issues in a balanced manner. Students will be assessed on their ability to analyse the question set with reference to the rights of patients; communicate their ideas, and formulate arguments and counter-arguments in an ethically justifiable manner.

- data interpretation of a graph that relates directly to healthcare practice, explanation of a numerical concept in simple, jargon-free language, and basic arithmetic without a calculator, which is an essential skill for a doctor to avoid making serious mistakes.

At Hull York Medical School there are three interviews including a group interview lasting 20 minutes.

'The main aim of this group activity at interview is to allow a 'live' assessment of your ability to work effectively with your peers. You will be scored on your level of contribution using a prescribed set of grade descriptors, by an experienced PBL tutor and one other trained assessor. In particular, we're interested in: your ability to work collaboratively in a group; how you contribute relevant information to the group discussion; and whether you articulate your own thoughts effectively and clearly in this setting.' – Hull York Medical School

At Lancaster the MMI consists of 10-12 different stations, most of which are 5 minutes long. Some of the stations consist of a short interview where you could be asked questions about your career choice, work experience or suitability for a medical career.

At others, you could be asked to read a short paragraph or watch a short video clip, take some notes and then discuss it at a subsequent station.

A 20-minute station involving group work is designed to assess your suitability for their problem-based learning curriculum.

In group interviews try to be a good team member by listening to others without interrupting or putting them down, whilst contributing effectively and enthusiastically without coming across as confrontational or domineering.

Above all, remember to be yourself and be friendly. If you don't agree with someone, try to put across your argument tactfully and praise others for their contributions.

Try to draw in quieter members of the group offering them openings to have their say. The interviewers are assessing how you get on with others as much as what you have to say so don't be too competitive or arrogant.

Breaking bad news is a common theme in role-play exercises and you must be able to show empathy whilst being honest about the situation.

It may be that someone's pet has just been killed or you may have to tell a 'patient' that they have cancer. Whatever the situation, make sure the other person is sitting down before explaining the bad news honestly, simply and clearly. Ask them if they understand what you are telling them and be prepared to repeat it in a different way.

Don't be surprised if the other person bursts into tears, in fact it might be a good idea to have a packet of tissues in your pocket or a clean handkerchief to offer them.

Don't be put off by this or try to stop them and don't tell them that everything will be alright if you have just told them they have a terminal illness for example. Instead ask them how they are feeling and acknowledge their feelings.

Use appropriate body language by nodding and using open gestures and don't be afraid of staying silent while they compose themselves if necessary.

'I had an MMI at one medical school, where there were 7 stations. We all had to wait in a corridor outside a closed door each, where we were given instructions to read before a bell went and we went in each room for 5 minutes. During the interviews I got confused over which door I was to go to next and lost valuable time so I didn't manage to read all the instructions before I went in for that interview. I had trouble answering all the questions but I still had to carry on with the other interview stations afterwards. When I came out I was exhausted and thought I'd done really badly but to my surprise I was offered a place a couple of months later, so you never know – always stay positive!' – 1st year medical student.

Chapter 13

After The Interview

Waiting for the result 150
Coping with rejection 150
Getting an offer 152
Health assessment and disclosure 153
Applying for funding 154
Scholarships and bursaries 156
Paying the money back 157
Getting the grades 157
Exam results 158
You made it! 159

Waiting for the result

The interview season generally lasts from October to March and a small number of applicants may hear the result shortly after their interview. However, the majority of applicants will have to wait for several weeks or months before they receive news. This can be incredibly frustrating but while you are waiting remember that no news is good news and get on with the job of getting those necessary grades. After months of voluntary work and weeks of work experience, this is the time to focus on your upcoming exams and get as much study in as possible. It's no good if you get an offer and then miss out on the grades.

Coping with rejection

It is quite common for applicants to be rejected from one or more of their medical school choices either before or after interview. Try not to get disheartened if this happens to you, after all you only need one offer. However, some applicants may find that they are unsuccessful in all four of their choices despite being highly academic all-rounders with a wealth of work experience simply because of the competitive nature of the process. There are simply not enough places for the number of applicants, which rises each year.

If this happens to you, don't take it personally. Instead look carefully at your application and try to work out where you were unsuccessful.

Phone the admissions office of the medical schools you applied to and ask politely for some feedback from them. They may or may not be helpful, but it is definitely worth asking.

If you failed to receive an interview, there may have been a problem with either your grades (actual or predicted) or your personal statement or school reference. Check through the medical school's website and make sure you met their GCSE subject and grade requirements; your A level choices were suitable; and your AS results were good enough. Then read your personal statement. Did you really sell yourself? Did you reflect enough on your work experience and relate your attributes and skills to medicine? Ask your teacher or referee if you can look over their reference too.

If you were invited to interview but failed to get an offer then you will need to reflect on your performance at interview. Did you prepare answers to predictable questions adequately? Could you have come across as unmotivated or arrogant?

Now you have to decide what to do next. The most important thing you should do is talk to other people about your options. Teachers can be helpful as they can take a more objective view than your parents or family. You may have an offer for a non-medical subject and decide to accept that and then possibly re-apply as a graduate in three years time. Or you may decide to take a gap year and reapply next year, or if your grades weren't good enough, look into other career options.

Remember that many medics failed to get into medical school the first time and still make excellent doctors. A year spent working in a healthcare setting may be what you need to show your determination and motivation to succeed, or a few months travelling or working abroad may help you to re-evaluate your reasons for studying medicine.

Getting an offer

For most medical schools about half of the applicants will receive an invitation to interview and then about half of those interviewed will receive a conditional offer, but this is a generalisation and actual universities may differ especially if they are particularly popular.

For 2014 entry to Hull York Medical School there were 1,296 home applications received. 1,052 of these met the entry requirements and 623 applicants were interviewed. From those 329 home offers were made.

If you do receive an offer, you have done incredibly well to make it through the whole application process and you should definitely celebrate! Even if it is not your first choice university, at least you are on your way to medical school (there is just the small hurdle of getting the grades left).

You will be notified that you have an offer through UCAS Track and you should also receive an email from the university, either before your Track changes or after.

You do not have to accept the offer until you have heard from all 4 of your choices; don't think that there is any hurry. However, if you are lucky enough to receive offers from your top two choices, then you can choose to accept them both, one as a firm offer and one as insurance. Your other two choices will automatically be declined, even if you are still waiting for a result and you will be freeing up two more potential places to other applicants.

It is unusual for an applicant to receive offers from all 4 of their choices, so if that happens to you, well done! You must have done a fantastic job! It is more usual to receive just one or two offers, so don't be disheartened if you receive some rejections as well. That is normal!

Health assessment and disclosure

When you have received an offer, you will probably be sent a health assessment form and disclosure. All students must comply with the Department of Health's guidance on health clearance for healthcare workers. Early clinical contact means that students will be asked to provide proof of their immunisation status on entry, so make sure all your immunisations are up-to-date.

Immunity against the following diseases is required: polio, tetanus, varicella (chickenpox), diphtheria, measles, mumps, rubella and TB.

Applying for funding

As soon as you receive an offer from any of your university choices you should think about applying for funding. All English students who have been ordinarily resident in the UK for at least three years prior to starting their course should be eligible for a tuition fees loan of up to £9,000. There are also maintenance loans available from between £2,843 a year for students living at home and £3,575 for students living away (£4,988 for students based in London). These loans are repayable after graduation, once the student is earning above a threshold. There are also top-up loans and grants available for some students, depending on their family income.

Scottish students studying in Scotland will get a non-repayable grant for their tuition fees, but Scottish students studying outside Scotland will only be eligible for a repayable loan.

Students from Northern Ireland studying in Northern Ireland will only be charged a maximum of £3,575 a year and should be eligible for a loan. If they study outside Northern Ireland, they will have to get a loan to pay tuition fees up to £9,000.

Welsh students studying anywhere in the UK will be eligible for a loan of £3,575 and a grant from the Welsh government to cover the balance up to £5,425.

You can apply for funding online and it will take about half an hour to complete the information. Make sure you have your passport details and national insurance number to hand.

If you want to get a maintenance loan you will need a UK bank account, although you can add the details of that later, if you prefer to wait and get a student bank account once you have started university.

If you think you are eligible for means-tested support, you will need to ask your parents to fill in the application with yo, and you may be asked to send photocopies of supporting documents like P60 forms, proof of income etc.

When you have completed the online application you will receive details of what you are eligible for, but you will only receive the first (out of three) instalment of your maintenance loan once you arrive at university.

Make sure you know exactly how much money you have and how long it should last for. Budgeting for the year is really important and it is useful to get your parents to help you with this.

Always make sure you let your parents know if you are experiencing difficulties with finance as the sooner problems are sorted out the better. There is also support available at the Student Advice Centres at each university.

During Fresher's week at university you will be offered plenty of student deals and discounts. When you open a bank account there may be an offer including a free student rail card or you may be offered a discount card that can be used in well-known shops and restaurants. However, make sure you have a bank account with a generous overdraft facility, or you may get a big shock if you go overdrawn. Whatever happens, don't be tempted to borrow money from payday loan companies, as these will charge extortionate fees on repayments.

Scholarships and bursaries

There are a variety of scholarships and bursaries available from individual universities and they will usually contact you with information once you have received an offer, so make sure you don't tick the box on the student finance form to opt out of sharing your financial information with the university.

There are also sponsorship schemes available from other sources, for example the Royal Navy. Other more obscure sources of funding include awards for vegetarians who have to promise not to eat meat at university and awards for children of chemists, grocers or travelling salesmen.

See the link below for more information:

http://www.telegraph.co.uk/education/universityeducation/student-finance/9834882/University-scholarships-10-unusual-student-bursaries.html

Paying the money back

Although the thought of accumulating debt can be scary, it is actually quite manageable, if you are sensible. You have to be earning over £21,000 a year before you pay back your loan, and if your salary drops below this, you can stop making repayments.

You will only pay 9% of your income on the amount over £21,000. So if you earn £25,000, you will pay 9% of £4000 per year.

You can choose whether to pay off your loan in 9% installments or all in one go, with no extra charge, and all repayments are taken out of your salary so you don't have to worry about missing a payment.

Getting the grades

Getting an offer doesn't mean you automatically have a place at medical school. You still have to achieve the grades offered, which is not as easy as it might appear.

However, having got through the difficult process of gaining an offer, you would be silly to throw it all away by not studying hard enough.

Do everything you can to keep on top of your work, especially coursework and start revising in plenty of time. Don't leave it to the last minute.

Exam results

At last the day has come when you will finally find out if you have made it to medical school. Hopefully, your hard work will have paid off and you will achieve the grades you need for university.

However, for those who just miss out on their predicted and hoped for grades, don't worry. Call the admissions office directly as soon as you receive your results; don't waste time crying, you need to ask if they will consider a lower grade and get in before they offer a spare place to someone else. It is really important, therefore, that you are available to get your results on the day they come out, and have access to a phone. It won't be easy to sort out a university place if you are on a beach in Thailand or the rainforest in South America!

If you think you need a re-mark, let the medical school know that you are requesting one, so that they hold onto your place and don't give it to someone else.

Then ask your school to submit a request to the exam board straightaway, as there are deadlines for requesting a re-mark. You will only have to pay for a re-mark if your grade is not changed. However, do be aware that there is a chance that your grade may move down as well as up.

If you believe you have mitigating circumstances, then you should gather evidence from school and doctors, and ask your school to liaise with the medical school on your behalf. This should only be done in very extreme circumstances and must be done as soon as possible.

If all else fails, think about applying for another course through clearing, and try again in three years time as a graduate applicant.

You will have to be very sure that this is what you want to do, however, as it can be a very expensive and long way to reach medical school, and there is still no guarantee that you will get a graduate place, as graduate entry is even more competitive.

You made it!

If you have achieved the grades you needed to get into the medical school of your choice, then congratulations! You've made it to medical school! I wish you the best of luck with your medical studies, and your future career as a doctor.

Appendix 1

Suggested timeline

Year 10

Choose your GCSE options so that you have the best chance of gaining top grades. Make sure you choose all 3 sciences and do maths, English Literature and English Language as these are all compulsory for medicine.

Year 11

As well as working hard to get the best results you can in your GCSEs, start to plan some medically-related work experience for a week after you finish your exams. This week of work experience is compulsory for most students, but you will be getting an edge, if you can arrange to work in a GP surgery, hospital, pharmacy or residential home. Make sure there are no age restrictions.

Arrange some voluntary work for next year.

Choose 4 subjects to study at AS level; don't forget to include Chemistry and/or Biology as well as at least one more maths or science subject to make sure you qualify for the majority of medical schools.

Year 12

This is your busiest year; not only do you have to get to grips with harder academic subjects, but you should be trying to volunteer outside school for a minimum of an hour each week.

During your half-term holidays try to organise as much shadowing or work experience as possible, whilst still keeping up with your studies.

At school, build up your responsibilities by offering to take on leadership roles like sports or house captain, mentoring or coaching younger students and also take part in team activities like Duke of Edinburgh or sport teams.

Revise hard for your AS exams as the results will be crucial to your application and after your exams visit as many university Open Days as you can.

During the summer holidays book and prepare for UKCAT or BMAT tests. Try to take the UKCAT as early as you feel possible to get it out of the way.

Reflect on your work experience and volunteering, then plan and draft your personal statement.

Year 13

Narrow down your choices of medical school to the four that suit you best.

Edit and check your personal statement so that it is ready to send to UCAS when the applications open.

Take the BMAT test, if applicable.

Continue to volunteer as much as possible.

Prepare for interviews so that you are ready when the invitations come in. Read the health news at least 3 or 4 times a week and keep up to date with current issues. Practise interview question and answers and build up a stock of stories to illustrate your strengths and weaknesses and anecdotes about different aspects of your work experience.

Finally, study hard and get your A grades!

Appendix 2

Medical school GCSE requirements

If you have already completed year 11 and have your GCSE results, then look at the individual universities' GCSE (or equivalent) criteria below for guidance. However, be sure to double check on their websites, as they can change at any time.

Aberdeen University

SQA - AAAAB to be achieved in five Highers taken together in S5 at the first sitting. Chemistry is required to grade B minimum. Two subjects are required from Biology/Human Biology, Maths & Physics. Two further Highers in most other subjects. If one of the required subjects is not undertaken in S5 due to school policy or very exceptional personal difficulties, supporting documentation must be supplied and sent directly to the Medical Admissions Office when application is submitted.

GCSE - Grade C Passes in English and Maths are required. Biology is recommended; Physics is recommended (or Dual Award Science). A combination of Grade A & B passes at GCSE is expected, especially in science subjects.

Barts

All eligible applicants must have the following subjects at GCSE level, at grades AAABBB or above (in any order) to include Biology (or Human Biology), Chemistry, English Language and Mathematics (or Additional Mathematics or Statistics). The Science double award may substitute all sciences at GCSE.

University of Birmingham

Preference will be given to those applicants offering A* grades in Mathematics, English and Science subjects. Integrated Science (double certificate) is acceptable as an alternative to single sciences and overall GCSE performance will be considered.

Brighton and Sussex Medical School

We are primarily interested in the A and A* grades at GCSE and so the more of these you have the better. However, strong AS grades (where appropriate) will compensate for a weaker GCSE profile. Please note that, for all applicants, we expect grades B in GCSE Maths & English (or their equivalent). Re-taken grades or equivalent qualifications are acceptable as evidence of adequate literacy and numeracy.

Bristol University

Subjects required at GCSE or equivalent: minimum five GCSEs at grade A to include Mathematics, English Language and two science subjects

Cambridge University

Students wishing to study Medicine must have achieved grade C or above in GCSE (or equivalent) Double Award Science and Mathematics. Two single awards in GCSE Biology and Physics may be substituted for Double Award Science.

Cardiff University

GCSEs in Mathematics B, English Language B and Sciences AAB or AA (Double Award). As a guide we advise applicants that you will need to achieve four to five A* in 9 GCSEs for your application to meet the minimum threshold, which is set each year once all applications are received.

Please remember that we have to include your Maths, English Language and Sciences grades in those 9, even if you have higher grades in other subjects. Once we have looked at our required subjects, we will then look at your top grades from your remaining GCSEs. Our maximum score possible is 27.

Dundee University

SQA - A minimum group of AAABB grades at SQA Higher level will allow consideration. The subjects must include Chemistry and another Science subject, all to be obtained at the same sitting. The other three Highers can be your own choice and this choice of subjects will not influence the assessment. We also require Biology at least to Standard Grade. Applications supported by AAAAC grades from 5th year will also be considered, provided the C grade is not in Higher Chemistry. (Approx. 6% of candidates sitting 5 Highers attain these grades). Achievement at standard grade will also be taken into account.

GCSE - Achievement at GCSE and AS level will also be taken into account.

Biology is required, at least to GCSE level.

Durham University

If only one of Biology and/or Chemistry is offered at A or AS level, the other should be offered at GCSE grade A (or Dual Award Science grade A). Once the academic criteria have been met, academic achievement is not considered further in subsequent parts of the application process, eg additional A levels or A* results or additional GCSE results are not considered.

University of East Anglia

All applicants must have a minimum of six GCSE passes at grade A or above to include English, Mathematics and two Science subjects.

GCSE short courses are not accepted. When considering your application we will usually review your best 8 results (to include English, Mathematics and two sciences, as above). A maximum of three Science GCSE subjects will be considered within the top 8 scoring GCSEs. Repeat GCSEs are accepted.

University of Edinburgh

SQA Highers - AAAAB in one sitting, normally in S5, to include Chemistry and two of Biology, Mathematics or Physics. For some applicants this subject combination at S5 Higher is neither possible nor appropriate. Students who meet the grade requirements in S5 but are missing one or more sciences may take the missing subject(s) in S6. Human Biology may replace Biology. Standard Grades: Standard Grade Credit (or Intermediate 2 at Grade B) in Biology, Chemistry, English and Mathematics.

GCSEs - Grade B in Biology, Chemistry, English, Mathematics. Double Award combined sciences or equivalent at Grade BB may replace GCSE grades in sciences. Additional Applied Science and Applied Science will not be accepted. All examination grades must be obtained at the first attempt of each subject. Those applying with resit qualifications (other than two GCE AS Level modules) will not be entered into the selection system unless under very exceptional circumstances (for which verified evidence has been provided prior to UCAS application).

Exeter University

You will need to show evidence of acceptable levels of literacy and, where applicable, numeracy. This is normally evidenced by GCSE English and GCSE Mathematics with a minimum pass of Grade C. Higher grades may be specified for individual programmes of study.

Glasgow University

Applicants are required to achieve AAAAA or AAAABB by the end of S5 at the first sitting, including Chemistry and Biology, and either Maths or Physics. Applicants must have English at either Grade 2 Standard Grade or an Intermediate 2. It is acceptable to take Biology/Chemistry/Maths or Physics as a crash Higher in S6 provided Grades AAAAA or AAAABB are achieved by the end of S5. A minimum of Grade B would be required in any crash Higher subject studied in S6. Biology and Human Biology are considered as equal subjects.

Hull York Medical School

GCSE English Language at grade A. We will accept grade B only if you have GCSE English Literature at grade A, or you are a school-leaver and you have AS-level or A-level English Literature or English Language at grade B. GCSE Maths at grade A. We will accept grade B only if you are a school-leaver and you have AS-level or A-level Maths at grade B. Six other GCSEs at grades A-C.

Imperial College London

All applicants must have the following subjects at GCSE level, at grades AAABB or above (in any order) Biology (or Human Biology), Chemistry, English Language, Mathematics (or Additional Mathematics or Statistics), Physics. The Science double award may substitute all sciences at GCSE.

Keele University

We require a minimum of four GCSE subjects at grade A, not including short-course GCSEs. Mathematics, English Language, Biology, Chemistry and Physics must be passed at a minimum of grade B. GCSE Science/Core Science (including AQA Science A or Science B) plus Additional Science is acceptable as an alternative to Biology, Chemistry and Physics. If Further Additional Science has been taken, this must also be passed at grade B. IGCSE double-award Science is also acceptable. Applied Science is not an acceptable GCSE.

King's College London

GCSE requirement: at least grade B at English Language and Maths, if not offered at A/AS-level.

Lancaster University

In nine subjects attained by the end of year 11 you must score at least 15 points from the nine. (A* or A = 2 points; B = 1 point) At least grade B in the following required subjects- Biology, Chemistry, and Physics (or Core & Additional Science) English Language and Mathematics. All other subjects must be at least grade C.

University of Leeds

We expect candidates to have obtained a substantial number of GCSE passes, at a high standard. At least 6 grade Bs must be offered including English, Maths, Dual Science/Double Science, or Chemistry and Biology.

University of Leicester

We do not specify a minimum number of A*grades at GCSE. However, we may need to take GCSE performance into consideration when selecting candidates for interview as competition for our places is so intense.

Applicants must have achieved at least a grade C in English Language, Mathematics and Double Science.

University of Liverpool

Evidence of excellent attainment in general secondary education. GCSEs in nine subjects attained by the end of Year 11 and at least a score of 15 points (where A*/A = 2; B = 1) from the nine and including Core & Additional Science (or Biology, Chemistry, and Physics), English Language, and Mathematics (all at least grade B). Two points is the maximum score awarded in each subject area. (e.g. Only one of Maths and Further Maths will be considered and 2 points at most will be available for Dual Award GCSEs except for Dual Science for which up to 4 points may be awarded). Short course GCSEs will at most receive half the points of a full GCSE but two short courses can be offered in place of a full GCSE. Preference will be given to applicants with a higher GCSE score.

University of Manchester

At least seven subjects are required at grade C or above; at least five must be at A or A*. English Language and Mathematics are required at GCSE minimum grade B. All applicants are expected to adhere to these GCSE requirements. If you are resitting any GCSE subjects, you must explain the extenuating circumstances that prompted this. Physics and Biology are required either at AS or at GCSE at minimum grade C. (Chemistry is essential at A2). If Dual Award Science or Core and Additional Science are offered, the minimum required is BB. In Grade A requirements, the School does not currently accept Applied ICT, Applied Business, short courses or BTEC qualifications.

Newcastle University

If only one of Biology and/or Chemistry is offered at A or AS level, the other should be offered at GCSE grade A (or Dual Award Science grade A). Once the academic criteria have been met, academic achievement is not considered further in subsequent parts of the application process. e.g additional GCSE results are not considered.

University of Nottingham

A minimum of 6 grade As at GCSE to include biology, chemistry and physics (or science double award). A minimum of grade B in maths and English language. Grade A at AS level physics can compensate for achieving grade B at GCSE.

Oxford University

There are no GCSE requirements, but in order to be adequately equipped for the BMAT and for the academic demands of the course, and if Biology, Physics or Mathematics have not been taken to A-level (or equivalent), applicants will need to have received a basic education in those subjects (for example at least a grade C at GCSE, Intermediate 2 or Standard grade (Credit), or equivalent; the GCSE Dual Award Combined Sciences is also appropriate).

Plymouth University

Applicants need to achieve 7 GCSE passes at grades A-C which must include English Language, Mathematics and either GCSE Single and Additional Science or GCSE Biology and Chemistry.

Queen's University Belfast

The best 9 GCSEs will be considered with 4 marks for an A star and 3 for an A. Maximum 36 points.

Sheffield University

You must have GCSE passes at grade C or above in Mathematics, English and the Sciences (which may be dual awards). You should have at least six A grades in GCSE subjects.

Southampton University

A minimum of seven GCSEs at grade A, including mathematics, English and double award science (or equivalent). You may offer qualifications which are equivalent to GCSE.

St. Andrews University

From experience of applications in previous years it would appear that to be competitive, applicants with A Levels require a minimum of 8 A grades at GCSE (to include Maths and Sciences) to be taken at one sitting and predictions of A*AA at A level.

St. George's University

416 tariff points from the top eight subjects at GCSE (equivalent to an average of grade A). Subjects must include English Language (minimum grade B), Maths and Dual Award or the three separate sciences. This is the points system we use: A* 58, A 52, B 46, C 40, D 34, E 28. We will only accept a complete set of scores from one sitting.

UCL

GCSE at grade B or above in both English Language and Mathematics. A foreign language (other than Ancient Greek, Biblical Hebrew or Latin) at GCSE grade C or equivalent. Candidates may be admitted if they do not offer a foreign language at GCSE, but they would be obliged to take an additional language course during their first year or to attend a language summer school.

Appendix 3

How universities use the UKCAT

Below are some of the universities, which require the UKCAT test, showing how they use the results:

University of Aberdeen

Candidates' UKCAT scores are considered in our selection for interview but are not the sole indicator for selection. They are considered alongside actual and predicted academic achievement and the objective scoring of information supplied on the UCAS application form (the Personal Statement and Reference). All indicators are considered together in deciding who will be selected for interview. A minimum UKCAT cut-off score is NOT used. Applicants to Aberdeen offer a broad range of UKCAT scores. For 2013 entry the lowest total score for an applicant was 1500 and the highest 3260. The lowest total score for successful applicants who were made offers was 2140 and the highest 3230.

Cardiff University

We do not use a strict threshold; your UKCAT score will be used in conjunction with a range of other academic and non-academic assessments as part of the selection process.

University of Dundee

Your UKCAT score will be factored into the pre-interview rank. There is no specific cut off applied but obviously a high score is advantageous. Our analysis of the 2013 applicants revealed the average calculated from applications received was 2520 and the average for those gaining offers was 2720.

University of East Anglia

While we include consideration of your Cognitive UKCAT score within our selection process. WE DO NOT HAVE A CUT OFF VALUE.

University of Edinburgh

Once all the scores are received we rank them, divide the groups into quartiles and allocate a score. The points are then added to your total score to contribute towards your final ranking.

University of Exeter

Applications will be sorted according to academic profile and overall UKCAT score in order to determine which applicants will receive an offer of an interview.

University of Glasgow

Interviewees who meet/are predicted to achieve the minimum academic entry requirements will be ranked by UKCAT total score. Allocations for interviews will then be processed from the top UKCAT total score.

Hull York Medical School

If you meet our academic entry requirements, score above 2800 in UKCAT with at least 450 in each subtest, we invite you to interview. Otherwise, we award you a number of points depending on your UKCAT score, and add this to the points from your UCAS form to give the total score which we use to rank you against other applicants. If you have a total UKCAT score of less than 2400, we won't normally consider your application. Furthermore, if you scored less than 450 in any subtest, we won't normally consider your application. If you meet these minimum requirements, your UKCAT score contributes to your application as follows:

UKCAT score	Outcome
less than 2400	we won't consider your application
2400-2599	+10pts
2600-2699	+15pts
2700-2799	+20pts
2800+	+25pts

Keele University

Use UKCAT results only in borderline cases: for students with the highest level of academic achievement or highest-scoring personal statements, the UKCAT score will not be taken into account. Those applicants who narrowly miss achieving the required score for their UCAS application may receive further consideration on the basis of their UKCAT score. In these borderline cases, the required UKCAT score will depend upon the level of performance in the test among this group of applicants; however, it is unlikely that applicants with total UKCAT scores below 2,400 will be successful at this stage. Applicants holding offers who narrowly miss achieving the required grades in their A-levels (or equivalent level-3 qualification) may receive further consideration if there are places available. In these circumstances, the factors taken into consideration in allocating remaining places will include interview score and UKCAT score.

University of Manchester

To help identify talented students from all backgrounds, UKCAT scores from UK candidates who come from similar educational and socio-demographic backgrounds are considered against each other. This is done by using supplemental information provided by publicly available datasets. Equal proportions of top scoring applicants from each group are then selected for interview.

University of Newcastle

The UKCAT threshold may differ in each admissions cycle as it is dependent on the scores achieved by those applicants who apply to our Medical School in the current cycle. Last cycle the cut-off score was 2780 with an average score of 695 on each module.

University of Nottingham

We will score the following areas of your application:
- Highest eight GCSEs (including the three sciences or the science double award, maths and English language)
- Results from the online questionnaire
- Each of the four cognitive sections of the UKCAT (verbal reasoning, quantitative reasoning, abstract reasoning and decision analysis)

The scores from the three areas are totalled together (this covers most of our applicants). The 50% of applicants with the highest scores are considered further and will have their personal statement and reference scored and added to the previous scores. We will interview around 600 applicants who achieved the highest total scores.

Plymouth University

UKCAT test results will be used, alongside the academic information contained on your UCAS form to select direct school leavers for interview. You will be required to meet a minimum standard in each of the four subtests, plus meet an overall target score which is set and reviewed annually by the Admissions Advisory Panel.

Queen's University Belfast

All applicants will take the UKCAT and their overall score will attract up to six points. This score will be added to their knowledge based mark and all applicants ranked.

The top circa 500 applicants will then be considered under stage 2 of the selection process, which will be a nine station multiple mini interview (MMI) to determine non-cognitive performance.

University of Sheffield

It is likely that any candidate with a score of 2600 or above will be given consideration.

University of Southampton

All applicants to BM4 and BM5 programmes must score 2500 or above in the UKCAT exam in order for their application to be considered further. The Faculty of Medicine will then be ranking applicants by UKCAT score and a certain percentage will be invited to attend a selection day.

University of St Andrews

At St Andrews we use the UKCAT in two ways: Firstly we set a cut off for the overall UKCAT score and applicants obtaining a score below that will not be considered for interview or a medical place. We have a limited number of interview places (around 500). Many more than 500 of our applicants offer a strong academic performance and excellent personal statement and reference. Therefore, to decide which of those strong applicants should get an interview, we use the global UKCAT score. The cut-off level depends on the number of strong applicants each year and the number of interview places available. A cut off score for each admissions cycle will be decided upon once all applications have been assessed.

Secondly, at St Andrews the UKCAT score will be used as part of an applicant's overall ranking following interview. The UKCAT score will be worth 15% of an overall admissions score. That percentage will be generated by a points system whereby applicant scores will be ranked and divided into bandings with points allocated per banding.

In order to be competitive and obtain an offer, a high score would be advantageous. The average global UKCAT score for UCAS applicants who obtained an offer for 2013 entry was 2740.

St George's, University of London

Applicants must achieve a minimum of 500 in each section of the UKCAT test. In addition, a total overall UKCAT score must be met; this is set after the application closing date when the UKCAT results are released. For 2014 entry, the minimum overall score, required to be selected for interview, was 2590 with a minimum score of 500 in each of the 4 sections of the test. For 2013 entry, the overall score was 2530. We select the top 600 for interview.

University of Warwick (Graduate Entry)

A score is allocated for the full distribution of the UKCAT scores of applicants. Applicants achieving a UKCAT score of 90th centile or greater are normally invited to the Selection Centre, subject to a review of their UCAS form and personal statement. Applicants with only a first degree and a UKCAT score below the 60th centile; a Masters and a UKCAT score below the 40th centile; or a PhD and a UKCAT score below the 20th centile are excluded without screening of their UCAS form and personal statement. For all other applicants (including those who are UKCAT exempt) the full scoring system (i.e. including an assessment of the UCAS form and personal statement) will be used. Of these, the highest scoring group will be invited to the Selection Centre (the number invited to the Selection Centre is normally in the region of 380-440)

Appendix 4

Useful university contact information

University of Aberdeen Medical School
T: +44 (0) 1224 272000
E: medadm@abdn.ac.uk

Barts and The London School of Medicine & Dentistry
T: +44 (0) 20 7882 8478 / 2243
E: smdadmissions@qmul.ac.uk

University of Birmingham Medical School
Admissions Tutor: Dr Austen Spruce
T: +44 (0) 121 414 6888
E: medicineadmissions@contacts.bham.ac.uk

Brighton and Sussex Medical School, University of Sussex
Undergraduate admissions enquiries
T: +44 (0) 1273 643528 / 643529 / 641966
E: medadmissions@bsms.ac.uk

University of Bristol Medical School
Medical Admissions Advisor
T: +44 (0) 117 928 7679 or +44 (0) 117 928 7677
E: med-admissions@bristol.ac.uk

University of Cambridge Medical School
Undergraduate admission enquiries
T: +44 (0) 1223 333308
E: admissions@cam.ac.uk

Cardiff University School of Medicine
T: +44 029 20 68 8113
E: medadmissions@cardiff.ac.uk

University of Durham
T: +44 (0) 191 334 0353
E: medicine.admissions@durham.ac.uk

University of East Anglia
Course enquiries
T: +44 (0) 1603 591515
E: enquiries@uea.ac.uk

University of Edinburgh College of Medicine
Undergraduate admissions enquiries
T: +44 (0) 131 242 6407
E: medug@ed.ac.uk

University of Exeter Medical School
Undergraduate admissions
T: +44 (0) 1392 725500
E: ug-ad@exeter.ac.uk

University of Glasgow School of Medicine
Admissions enquiries
T: +44 (0) 141 330 6216
E: med-sch-admissions@glasgow.ac.uk

Hull-York Medical School, University of York
Undergraduate Admissions
T: +44 (0) 1904 321782
E: admissions@hyms.ac.uk

Imperial College London Faculty of Medicine
Admissions Team
T: +44 (0) 20 7594 7259
E: medicine.ug.admissions@imperial.ac.uk

Keele University School of Medicine
T: +44 (0) 1782 733937
E: admissions.ukeu@keele.ac.uk

King's College London School of Medicine
T: +44 (0) 207 848 7964/ 7965/ 7963
E: ug-healthadmissions@kcl.ac.uk

Lancaster Medical School
Admissions Office
T: +44 (0) 1524 594547
E: medicine@lancaster.ac.uk

University of Leeds School of Medicine
Admissions Team
T: +44 (0) 113 343 2336
E: ugmadmissions@leeds.ac.uk

University of Leicester College of Medicine
Senior Admissions Tutor
T: +44 (0) 116 252 2969
E: med-admis@le.ac.uk

University of Liverpool School of Medicine
Admissions Team
T: +44 (0) 151 795 4370
E: chb@liv.ac.uk

University of Manchester Medical School
Undergraduate admissions office
T: 44 (0) 161 275 5025 / 5774
E: ug.medicine@manchester.ac.uk

Newcastle University Medical School
Administrator for Admissions
T: +44 191 208 7005
E: medic.ugadmin@ncl.ac.uk

University of Nottingham
T: +44 (0) 115 823 0000
E: enquiries@nottingham.ac.uk

University of Oxford
Pre-Clinical Medicine Enquiries
T: +44(0) 1865 285788
E: admissions@medschool.ox.ac.uk

Peninsula College of Medicine and Dentistry
T: +44 (0) 1752 437444
E: info@pcmd.ac.uk

Queen's University Belfast School of Medicine
T: +44 (0) 28 9097 3838
E: Intl.Student@qub.ac.uk

University of Sheffield Medical School
T: +44 (0) 114 222 5533
E: medadmissions@sheffield.ac.uk

University of Southampton Medical School
T: +44 (0) 23 8059 4408
E: ugapply.fm@southampton.ac.uk

University of St Andrew's School of Medicine
T: +44 (0) 1334 461851
E: medicine@st-and.ac.uk

St George's University of London
T: +44 (0) 20 8725 2333
E: enquiries@sgul.ac.uk

UCL Medical School
T: +44 (0) 20 7679 0841
E: medicaladmissions@ucl.ac.uk

Printed in Great Britain
by Amazon.co.uk, Ltd.,
Marston Gate.